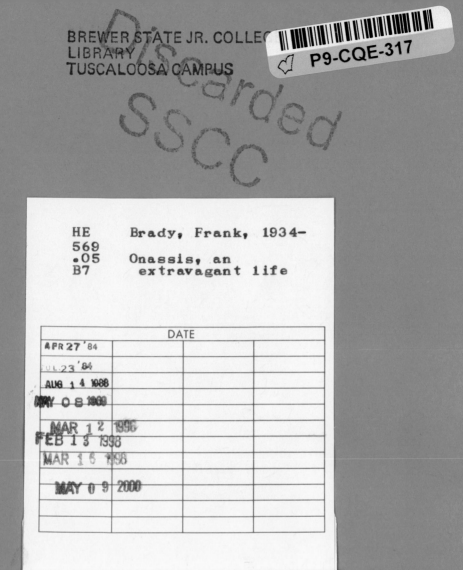

HE
569
.05
B7

Brady, Frank, 1934-

Onassis, an
extravagant life

DATE		
APR 27 '84		
JUL 23 '84		
AUG 1 4 1988		
MAY 0 8 1989		
MAR 1 2 1996		
FEB 1 3 1998		
MAR 1 6 1998		
MAY 0 9 2000		

Books by Frank Brady
ONASSIS
HEFNER
PROFILE OF A PRODIGY

ONASSIS

An Extravagant Life

Frank Brady

PRENTICE-HALL, INC., Englewood Cliffs, New Jersey

Onassis: An Extravagant Life, by Frank Brady
Copyright © 1977 by Frank Brady
Printed in the United States of America
Prentice-Hall International, Inc., London
Prentice-Hall of Australia, Pty. Ltd., Sydney
Prentice-Hall of Canada, Ltd., Toronto
Prentice-Hall of India Private Ltd., New Delhi
Prentice-Hall of Japan, Inc., Tokyo
Prentice-Hall of Southeast Asia Pte. Ltd., Singapore
Whitehall Books Limited, Wellington, New Zealand
10 9 8 7 6 5 4 3 2 1

Library of Congress Cataloging in Publication Data
Brady, Frank
    Onassis, an extravagant life.
    Includes index.
    1. Onassis, Aristotle Socrates, 1906-1975.
2. Merchant marine — Biography.   I. Title.
HE569.05B7   387.5'092'4   [B]   77-24418
ISBN 0-13-634378-3

to Maxine

1

Gethsemane Onassis gently woke her six-year-old grandson Aristotle by kissing him warmly all over his body, from his feet up to his head. The old woman smiled as the drowsy and blinking black-eyed child stood obediently on the bed; she helped him off with his linen nightshirt and began to wash him from an olive wood bowl of hot, soapy water. At his birth, it was she who had rubbed and cleansed Aristo, as he came to be known, with lukewarm wine and myrtle leaves. She had continued bathing, feeding and caring for him, always with the imprimatur of his mother, every day since then.

Downstairs, now dressed in short blue pants, black shoes, white shirt and crimson tie, Aristo sat in the bright blanched-walled kitchen drinking his bowl of hot milk and dreamily playing with the small squares of bread crusts that had been trimmed, especially to his preferred size, by the family cook. He picked at the kumquats also placed before him, ate one, and then went to the open window and looked out. Down a steep, silver-green slope smelling of mint and thyme, only a short distance from the vine-covered Onassis villa, lay the sea, the majestic Gulf of Smyrna; and beyond that, the hyacinthine waters of the Aegean.

At the turn of the century, sometime about 1901, a determined, ambitious young man named Socrates Onassis made the difficult, somewhat frightening decision to move from his home in Kayseri, in central Turkey, to the ancient city of Smyrna, located on the easternmost coast of Asia Minor and almost within touching distance of the liberated Greek islands of Chios, Lesbos and Samos. A Turkish citizen, Socrates' allegiance and philosophy were Greek. Although his ancestors had lived in Kayseri as merchants for centuries and spoke Turkish, they also spoke Greek, attended the Greek Orthodox church and followed Greek customs. As Turks of Greek descent, these 3,000,000 Anatolian "Hellenists" were apart from their countrymen and lived a special life afforded them by the sultans. There was a Greek sector in most large Turkish cities; they had their own schools and hospitals. Although sometimes persecuted by local Turkish potentates, they lacked a subjacent ghetto mentality, and considered themselves to be highly superior to the Turks. The Turks used their conquered subjects to expand and administer their finances and to staff the bureaucracy of the empire. Greeks rose to high offices in the service of the sultan and handled most of the Mediterranean trade. They were known as excellent businessmen, even though they were considered "outsiders" by the Turks, whose hatred would erupt in small ways on a daily basis. Like the Jews in many European cities, the Anatolians dominated the commerce of the areas in which they lived.

Although he left a large, close family of brothers, sisters, aunts, uncles and cousins, in addition to his mother and father, Socrates at 25 years of age moved to Smyrna for two compelling reasons. His childhood sweetheart, Penelope

Dologlu, had gone there with her parents one year earlier and he was eager to court and marry her. The fact that Smyrna was one of the largest and richest cities of all Asia Minor, with a much larger Greek population than Athens itself, also attracted him, for Socrates Onassis was determined to make a significant mark in the world of commerce.

Soon after arriving in the gnarled but charming streets of Smyrna, he propelled himself into the commerce of the city. At first, he worked as an apprentice for Bohor Benadava, a prominent Jewish merchant. After learning all the young man thought he needed to know about importing and exporting, he opened his own small export office. Buying odd lots of such commodities as cotton, raisins and figs, he used the money he had earned from working for Benadava and some money he had saved in Kayseri to make his first big purchases.

It was with tobacco, however, that he made his first important stride, buying some obscure but thoroughly first-rate Turkish blends and selling them not only to Greek manufacturers and distributors but to the Dutch, French and Italians, as well. His command of languages—self-taught for the most part and charged with special commercial meaning for the businessmen he dealt with—enabled him to operate with great advantage in a city as international as Smyrna. In addition to Greek and Turkish, he was fluent in French, could be understood in English and had a smattering of several other languages. He worked long hours, and according to one report by the Turkish government issued years later and based on accounts of people who knew him, "he was known as an absolutely honest man of great integrity of character." He began to make friends and contacts all over the city, in all of the different quarters including the Turkish, and this not only helped his business grow enormously, but eventually saved his life.

As his business prospered and his solvency appeared assured, Socrates became more confident that his proposal of marriage would be acceptable to the father of the woman he loved. Penelope Dologlu, then 17 years old, was amenable to accepting his hand. Both families readily gave their blessing

3

and the serious young couple were married in a Smyrnan church. In less than one year, a child was born in a comfortable villa that he had bought in an outlying district just two miles from Smyrna called Karatas. The child was a girl, whom they baptized Artemis. Two years after that, on January 20, 1906, during a period of warm weather called *alkyonidkes*, they had another child, this one a boy Aristoteles* Socrates Onassis. He was christened one week later. In keeping with their tradition, his mother and father had to remain outside the church. The infant was carried inside by his godparents where he was totally immersed three times in holy water, his nose and mouth held tightly closed, his head anointed with oil and his body covered with a layer of salt. When the salt was washed off, relatives threw money into the baptismal font; the money was kept by the midwife.

As their own names were of classical origin, Socrates and Penelope chose classical names for their children. This was done by most of the Greek minority in Asia Minor and in other foreign countries as well, to indicate their loyalty to their heritage.

The name of Socrates Onassis became well-known in all of Smyrna and in outlying districts, as he continued to buy the best tobacco he could afford from the plantations spread throughout Asia Minor. Turkish tobaccos, grown in a warm climate with rich well-drained soil, were known for their quality. Socrates began exporting them all over the world. By the time his son Aristotle had reached school age, Socrates' tobacco-export firm was the third largest business of any kind in the city. He had a strong relationship and unquestionable credit with the Imperial Ottoman Bank. In fact, he had financed and held mortgages on a number of smaller businesses. Although not a "millionaire," he lived as lavishly and securely as any modern corporate mogul and was one of the most prosperous citizens in the city of Smyrna, which at that time was, next to Istanbul, the richest city in Turkey.

As soon as the business seemed strong, he moved into a suite of large offices on Grand Vizier Han Street in the northwestern section of the city, near the railway station where

*Aristoteles was his baptismal name.

he would have easy access to the tobacco that arrived from the interior. In addition to a group of loyal employees who had been with him from the start, Socrates' younger brother, Homer, came from Kayseri and helped out with the business. His mother, Gethsemane, widowed, had come to the city to live with her son and daughter-in-law when their first child was born. Eventually, the rest of his brothers, John, Alexander and Basil, also settled in Smyrna and worked in other professions.

Surrounded by olive and lemon trees, the house at Karatas was only a short walk to the sea. It was as lovely and secluded as a vacation spot and became the gathering place for all of the Onassis clan. Aristo grew up surrounded by a legion of aunts, uncles and cousins with a constant round of weddings, christenings and birthday parties, and weekly gatherings of relatives and friends who came just to socialize. In the early evening, the adults would sit under the grape arbor at the side of the house and watch the children roll down and play on the hill and romp near the water. As it grew to be dark, they would call them in for a dinner of enormous baked beans called *gigantes*, a salad of pickled caper leaves, and a dessert of milk-rice. After the children were put to bed, the adults would continue sitting in the open air, listening to the gramophone, eating, singing and drinking *ouzo* and imported gin until well past midnight. Then, invariably, one of the more animated or intoxicated of the group would rise and do the *Zeybekiko*, a solo dance named after a non-Turkish tribe, the Zeybeks, living in the mountains near Smyrna. The dance was a lonely gesture of rebellion and freedom and a symbolic slap at the Turks, since the Zeybeks, who were brigands, were a thorn in the flesh of the Turkish government. It was called the Dance of the Eagle.

Although he loved his mother and was close to her as a child, Aristo was actually raised by his grandmother, a not-so-unusual occurrence where a Greek grandparent lives in the same house as her grandchildren. Like many Asian-born Greek women, Gethsemane spoke only Turkish, and therefore, Aristo learned to speak that language as well as his "native" Greek.

With a doting, outrageously affectionate grand-

5

mother, an older sister eager to watch out for him and teach him whatever she knew, a handsome and loving mother, and a prosperous and brilliant father as proud of his only son as a man could be, Aristo developed as a secure, highly confident child who related well to his family. Of all the people in his early life, however, he was closest to his grandmother.

Gethsemane Onassis was a deeply religious woman, selfeducated, independent and of simple tastes. She went to church every day of her life, was friendly with all of the deacons, made an annual Easter pilgrimage to Jerusalem and attempted to instill her religious fervor in both Aristo and Artemis. Above each child's bed was hung a Greek crucifix, the walls were covered with the relics from her journeys to Israel — holy pictures, small icons and statues of saints were spread throughout their room. As an adult, Onassis often recalled that as a child, his grandmother lectured him constantly on the rewards of virtue and the penalties of sin — not only instant retribution or gratification in this life, but eternal happiness in heaven if he were a good boy and damnation in hell if he were bad. Despite the moralizing which often had a stern tone, she was a master of indulgence as far as Aristo was concerned and delighted in his childhood conversations. She did everything possible to spoil him.

He grew even closer to his grandmother when his mother found it impossible, due to a sudden illness, to spend virtually any time with the child. Penelope experienced a prolonged period of depression and lethargy which was followed by severe nausea and vomiting. The diagnosis was a malfunctioning kidney and it was thought that only a delicate operation could save her. She was admitted to the French Hospital, the operation was performed, but her system was too filled with her own poison. Within a few days after she entered the hospital, she was dead of uremic poisoning at the age of 25.

Except to realize that something strange had occurred, Aristo was not really aware of what had happened when his mother died. In the days immediately following her death, the household was different in many ways, but nobody stopped to explain why. All of the furniture was removed from his parent's bedroom and he was not permitted to enter during

6

the time the body lay there. With their hair hanging down, his grandmother and other close female relatives were atypically dressed in white for mourning. All the mirrors were turned to the wall and draped in black; the doors and windows of the house were left wide open; groups of women shrouded in black kept up a constant wailing lamentation that went on for days — a rhythmic drone composed of expressions he did not quite understand—"How could you leave us?"; "Why did you go, you who were so young and fair?" His sister, Artemis, seemed more affectionate, more interested in playing with him down by the sea.

He was not kept from the funeral and saw his mother, in an open casket of black velvet and purple muslin, her head resting on a pillow of flowers and leaves from a lemon tree, as if she were asleep, being carried to the graveyard of the Church of St. Paraskevis' just a short distance from the house. To confuse things even more, after the burial, there was a huge party with cakes and sweets of all kinds. The adults drank alcohol and there was music far into the night.

It was sometime later before Aristo actually realized that his mother had died the day he had seen her carried in a box by the pall bearers. It was a loss deeply felt by him later in his life. Not only did Gethsemane then become a more important part of his life, but his relationship with Artemis became so close that the two children were practically insepa-rable and fiercely loyal and protective toward each other, a feeling that would continue for the rest of their lives.

Socrates was grief-stricken over the loss of his beauti-ful young wife, and he knew that it would be difficult to raise two children without the influence of a mother. A man with substantial wealth and stature in the community and a generous nature, he had no trouble finding a woman to be his mate. Eighteen months after the death of Penelope, Socrates married again and Helen Onassis, whom he had also known in Kayseri, became Aristo's stepmother. Helen related very well to her new home and her two stepchildren and years later Onassis remembered her fondly and with love, stating that she was a "sweet, lovely and obedient wife" to his father. Within a year of her marriage, Helen presented the family with a baby girl,

Aristo's half-sister Merope. Barely a year later, another girl Calirrhoe was born.

Making the trip into Smyrna with Artemis each day, always accompanied by either Gethsemane or a servant, Aristo attended a series of private schools. He was an excellent student. Not surprisingly, one of his best subjects was theology, since in addition to daily catechism and study in school, he was given intense theological instruction at St. Paraskevis' where he had become a choirboy under the influence, or perhaps insistence, of his grandmother. Although choir practice and religious instruction were not his favorite pastimes, many of the hymns and dirges stayed fixed in his memory over a half-century later.

Brought up in wealth, surrounded for the most part by doting women, Aristo as the first and only son, could have been considered the prototype of the overindulged scion of a rich family. They vacationed several weeks each year on the nearby island of Chios, one of the seven traditional birthplaces of Homer, and Aristo practically lived on and in the water. Although he never quite mastered the intricacies of handling a sailboat by himself, he became a strong and excellent swimmer and oarsman. He matured quickly, assumed a fascination with women before he even entered his teens, excelled in sports beyond his years—he became school champion at rowing—and, under the tutelage of his father, took an interest in business. As soon as Socrates felt his son was old enough to be trusted and could find his way through the city, he was enlisted as the company messenger boy, delivering tobacco samples and price quotations to potential buyers. J. Paul Getty, in his book *As I See It*, talks of sitting in his favorite cafe on bustling Front Street in the Smyrna of 1913, sipping Turkish coffee or raki, and of telling Aristotle Onassis about it many decades later when they were both "billionaires." "As a kid, I went by the cafe several times a day—yes, even in December, 1913," replied Onassis, thinking of his peregrinations as messenger and schoolboy.

Socrates attempted to instruct the boy in the nuances of his business and by the time Aristo was 12, he was working in the office at least a few hours each day, learning the intricacies of the tobacco-export trade.

Gethsemane, however, had other ideas for her grandson. Since he was the firstborn son, she had secretly hoped he would become a priest, rather than a merchant. For each business lesson scheduled by his father for Aristo, Gethsemane offered religious instruction. Although he was a willing and faithful catechism student, it was the world of commerce that attracted him the most. Socrates' religious involvement consisted of attending church only during the principal religious holidays, Christmas and Easter, and he never encouraged Aristo to participate.

Aristo's life became thoroughly involved with tobacco. He often and willingly went with his father to the nearby depot of the Aidin Railway Station to look at the offerings of the farmers. He learned all about curing, aging and fermentation. He was taught the basis for selecting the best Turkish plants — small, bright yellow, yellowish-green or yellowish-brown leaves; or the celebrated Latakia blend bought by his father occasionally and consisting of a blend of leaves, buds and flowers, so mild that they were exported for cigarette or pipe purposes only. For a period, Socrates also bought quantities of a slow-burning tobacco called Persica, suitable for the old hookah smokers of Smyrna and Istanbul and many of the other cities of eastern Turkey.

It was mainly with tobacco leaves for cigars that Socrates built his business, however, and he was constantly puffing away on a large, dark brown stogie, either for his own pleasure or as a daily testing of the state of the current export. Aristo, enjoying the symbol of maturity, started smoking them clandestinely when he was about twelve years old; when caught and challenged by his father, he insisted that he, too, was "testing" to see if the tobacco, ready to be shipped or purchased, was of sufficient quality. But Aristotle was too clever to continue to take cigars from his father's supply. He found a better way. Whenever he delivered bills or messages to the small manufacturers spread throughout the city, Aristo asked for, and received, samples of their finest cigars. Undoubtedly, the businessmen believed the cigars were for Aristo's father. If there were any extra cigars left over, after he had selected the

9

choice ones to smoke himself, he sold them to his friends.

At the age of 13, he entered the *Evangeliki Scholi*, (Evangelical High School), the famous eighteenth century Greek school of Smyrna, under British patronage, and proved to be an excellent student.

When he occasionally had problems with a particular field of study (the curriculum was quite difficult even for good students), a tutor was hired. In his father's determination to assure him an excellent education, Aristo had the opportunity of working with some of the best teachers in the city. Socrates knew the importance of knowing languages and stressed that. Onassis was expected to study several, not only his native Greek and Turkish. A fairly large percentage of the top graduates of *Evangeliki Scholi* were automatically accepted at Oxford or Cambridge, and after his first year in high school it was planned that upon graduation, Aristotle would move to England and attend Oxford—something both he and his father wanted. Gethsemane was deeply disappointed; she realized that her dream of seeing her beloved grandson in a priest's black flowing robes would never happen, now. Of more immediate concern to the family was the increasing talk of war and the military occupation of Smyrna, headed by a German general, Liman von Sanders, who was in charge of the Turkish forces. Liman Pasha, as the Turks called him, moved into a villa quite close to the Onassis home, and it was necessary for all the Greeks to show constant respect and deference to Von Sanders and his German officers, while they secretly despised them. Aristo, like all the other children, was forced to wear a fez to school.

In 1919, the Greek army occupied Smyrna, and Socrates became the treasurer of an organization called "Ameni," formed by local Greek residents of the city to give support to the Greek Army of Occupation. Homer and the other Onassis brothers became highly involved in another Greek patriotic organization. Their particular hero was Greek Premier Eleutherios Venizelos, a prominent Cretan nationalist, who achieved an overwhelming victory in the election of 1910 and who took command at a time when the people were depressed by the ineffectiveness of the old politicians.

10

It was against this increasingly tense backdrop that Aristotle spent his early teenage years. The image of the pubescent, short-statured Aristo, smoking a large cigar, dressed in short pants with his blue Eton cap (which replaced the fez when the Turks were driven out) and English-cut jacket, leaving school each afternoon and making his way to his father's office across town, might seem a humorous one, but no one who saw him, even as an exuberant young teenager, was ever tempted to laugh. His involvement with a dynamic business, and the influence of his vital and successful father, gave the young Aristo a sophistication that was well beyond his years.

Aside from business, from the age of 11 or 12, Aristo had a lusty interest in girls. Although he was forbidden to date, he often found time to meet a favorite, buy her a sweet and perhaps walk her from school to home.

Many decades later, Ingebord Dedichen, the daughter of a wealthy Norwegian shipowner, who was Onassis' companion, recalled that he had told her that his first attempt at a sexual liaison was at the age of 11, in the basement of the house at Karatas, with the family's laundress, an uneducated girl scarcely older than he. Helen came home unexpectedly, checked to see if the laundress was completing her chores and found her stepson upon a pile of soiled bed linens about to tamper with both his and the girl's virginity. The act was interrupted, of course; the poor laundress was dismissed, and Aristo was severely chastised by both Helen and Gethsemane. Socrates feigned indignation, but gave his maturing son the best advice he could muster. The fact that the boy wanted to experiment didn't really bother him, but Aristo's selection of a mere laundress was of concern to his father. "Never become involved with someone who can make you lose stature, if the relationship becomes known," he advised the boy frankly. "Sleep up." It was advice that Aristo took to heart and would later apply to his life over and over again. Meanwhile, Socrates, to mollify his mother and wife, hired an old lady—"with the face of a witch," as Onassis later described her—as a replacement for the tempting young laundress.

Aristo's interest in women, heightened by that brief

11

though incomplete encounter, now erupted into a fever, or at least an intoxication. The girls he became most closely associated with were Greek, but occasionally, without his family's knowledge or approval, he would make sport of being a man and spend time alone with *Turkala*, young Turkish girls, known as great beauties.

Within a few months after his first sexual episode, he found himself attracted to his French tutor, an attractive and buxom girl in her mid-twenties. Alone with her one summer afternoon, Aristo sensed that the girl was also attracted to him and he was ready to test his prowess. Her scant blouse, open at the neck because of the intense heat, spurred him on and his advances were accepted. Thereafter, for a period of about one year, each French lesson was accompanied by a session in bed. Onassis later revealed that his French improved markedly. Not only did he try to impress his teacher, but he never missed a session.

The city of Smyrna was in flames, the holocaust, one of the biggest in the world's history, was larger than the Great Fire of London in 1666 or the blaze that wrecked San Francisco in 1906.

Two hundred thousand refugees jammed the city. Most were lined up on the docks and quays of the waterfront, huddled against the advancing flames. Many had not eaten in days. There was an outbreak of typhoid. Shocked and exhausted, most of the people had lost the capacity for panic.

The harbor was packed with ships from many nations—France, Italy, Britain and the United States. Most had accepted all the survivors they could hold and were ready to sail, though they knew not where. Aggressive escapees of the flames swam to a nearby ship and attempted to climb aboard; they were beaten off or shot. Towers of Greek churches, the domes of the mosques, and the flat square roofs of the houses were silhouetted against a glowing mass of yellow, orange and crimson fire, as thick clotted coils of oily black smoke rose hundreds of feet into the sky. The glow of the dying city could be seen 150 miles away. Even a mile out to sea, the cries of the dying could be heard, intermixed with the frequent roar and clash of exploding ammunition stores, accompanied by the rattle of burning cartridges, which sounded like an intense infantry battle. The Turks put up concentration camps on the outskirts of the city.

At night, Aristotle Onassis worked his way through the flaming streets. Some were impossible to traverse not only because of the wreckage, but because of the stench from the mass of corpses along the avenues. Many were killed by the fire; many more had been executed by the Turks in the days immediately preceding the holocaust. Hundreds of Greek men were taken from their homes and made to sit in the streets as the Turkish soldiers went systematically from man to man, slitting their throats, reciting the word "Padisha"—sultan. This form of death saved ammunition; it was also particularly excruciating. The wives and daughters of the dead men were then raped and beaten, and those who refused to submit were immediately slaughtered.

Aristotle attempted to get from the south of the city to his father's office in the north, a distance of a few miles, in order to remove whatever valuables he could. Walking, sometimes crawling along the Rue Parallelle, it took him hours to go just a few blocks as he darted into doorways to hide from the Turkish patrols. All around him the fire raged and the heat was so furious that the cobblestone streets appeared to melt into small rivers. There was constant shooting, followed by screams and panic-stricken running. The Turks were openly looting the entire city.

Aristotle hid in the bushes of a church. Nearby, a Greek priest was stripped of his garments and then blinded with a red-hot sword. The man was dragged to the large

14

doors of the church and soldiers crucified him by nailing horseshoes to his hands and feet. He died shortly afterwards. Aristotle realized that it was the same church where his mother and father were married.

Aristotle Onassis' developing years were inextricably intertwined with war. At the beginning of World War I, a time that found Greece divided, he was eight years old. The Greeks, in Asia Minor, although outwardly paying lip service to the Turks who had joined the Central Powers of Germany, Austria-Hungary and Bulgaria, were secretly loyal to the Western Allies, especially Great Britain and France.

With the advent of the Gallipoli Campaign to free the Dardanelles, Greece's premier, Venizelos, saw an opportunity to realize the dream of a Greek empire based in Constantinople, hence, the Greco-Turkish War of 1919-1922. At the Peace Conference in Versailles, Venizelos obtained the Supreme Council's permission, even encouragement, to occupy Smyrna, thereby gaining a foothold in Asia Minor.

The invasion of Asia Minor by the Greeks, however, provoked a resurgence of nationalism in Turkey. Mustafa Kemal, a brilliant and cruel Turkish general, lured the Greeks deep into Asia Minor, and finally, after months of evasive action, his forces encountered the exhausted Greeks at the Sokarya River and attacked the center of the Greek army at Dumlu Punar, a plateau 200 miles west of Smyrna. The crack Turkish troops began a successful rout, forcing the Greeks to retreat to Smyrna. As they retreated, the Greek troops plundered, looted and murdered the Turkish population in their flight, leaving a trail of violence that incensed the Turks almost into insanity as they went from village to village, finding not a house standing, and in some cases not a single survivor in an entire town.

As the Turkish soldiers entered towns populated by Greek civilians, they took their revenge. Radio reports and eyewitness accounts of the horror began to filter to Smyrna and reached there shortly before the first retreating troops entered the city.

Socrates Onassis had little time to solidify his position or make adequate preparations for the Turkish onslaught. His offices were shuttered, some valuables removed and he gathered his family around him in the house at Karatas. Although he knew it was dangerous to remain in Smyrna, he was convinced that his standing in the community and his many Turkish friends would help him. His brother Homer took no chances, however, and immediately fled the city to unknown parts.

On the 9th of September, 1922, the Turks reached and occupied Smyrna. For almost two weeks, the Greek soldiers, together with hundreds of thousands of Greek civilians, had been pouring into the city, attempting to evade the ravishing Turks who were now retaliating by slaughtering any Greek, young or old, male or female, they could capture. It was believed that the Greek army would attempt a defense of Smyrna but, knowing they were overwhelmingly outnumbered, they fled via the sea to Greece by the tens of thousands, including thousands of wounded, unaware perhaps that the Turks would have their vengeance realized, if not against the army, then against the Greek population.

Encouraged by their officers, the Turkish troops began to kill systematically. Wooden churches, packed with refugees, were set afire with benzine and those inside who were not burned alive were bayoneted if they attempted to escape. The fierce and bloody carnage was unequaled in modern history. As soon as a southeast wind began to blow, Turkish soldiers carrying tins of paraffin went from building to building and began to ignite the structures. The flames blew westward into the Greek sections, away from the Moslem area. Within a short time, the city, with the exception of the Turkish quarter, was engulfed in flames. A regiment of Turkish troops circled the city to prevent any of the refugees from escaping. By the 15th of September, six days after the Turkish occupation of Smyrna, 4,500 homes and shops were reduced to ashes and over 120,000 persons had died.

The complications of moving the remaining Greeks out of Turkey were vast — eventually, 1,500,000 refugees would be a part of that exodus. The Turks moved swiftly, not only in their wholesale massacre and deportation, but in the complete takeover of the workings of the smoldering city. All government buildings that were still standing were occupied, hotels were converted into barracks for the troops, and choice houses were commandeered by the top officers. The Onassis villa, which was one of the largest and most comfortable in the outlying district, was immediately inspected. One particular Turkish general remembered it from the years when he served as a colleague to Liman Pasha, a neighbor of Onassis, and he had preferred its direct, unhindered view of the sea just three hundred yards away. The dwelling was his during the war. When Socrates objected strenuously to the loss of his house, he could have easily been executed. However, the general didn't stoop to the same barbarism as his troops. He already had a complete intelligence report on Socrates Onassis and it was clear that he was not only a Greek sympathizer in every way, but a potentially dangerous political activist. Socrates was placed under arrest and imprisoned in the Cunak, the major jail deep within the Turkish quarter of the city. Within a short time, Aristo received a report that his Uncle Alexander had also been arrested, sentenced to death, and was hung in a public square in the city of Kasaba, 40 miles from Smyrna. His uncles Basil and John were placed in the equivalent of a concentration camp somewhere in Turkey, their exact location unknown. Socrates' sister, Marie, had sought refuge with hundreds of others in a church in the old Greek city of Akkissar, and together with her child and husband, was burned to death when the Turks set fire to it. Anyone who attempted to escape was bayoneted. No one survived.

As soon as Socrates had been incarcerated, Gethsemane, Helen, and Aristo's three sisters were sent to evacuation camps to await eventual passage to Greece. Only Aristo was permitted to remain in the house after its occupation by the Turkish officers, this for their own convenience and benefit. He spoke impeccable Turkish, knew his way around the city, was familiar with the workings of the villa and had many contacts that could prove to be useful. "I begged the general for permission to sleep there," Onassis related years later. "I knew how the plumbing and heating worked and I offered to run errands, too."

By the time of the Turkish takeover of Smyrna,

Aristotle Onassis was no longer a child; he was just short of 17 and had been readying himself to attend Oxford. In most Greek families, males were considered to be adults when they reached the age of 15 or 16 and were expected to perform the tasks, however demanding, associated with adulthood. When they were not attending school, young men were supposed to work, preferably with their fathers, as Aristotle had done for years. In the case of an absent or dead father, the oldest son was automatically considered the head of the family. After his father's imprisonment, Aristotle assumed the duties and burdens of this position with seriousness and dedication.

His first responsibility was to attempt to have his father released from prison, then to try to salvage what was left of any assets, and finally to do what he could to unite the family on the mainland of Greece. Traveling around the city was difficult, because of the destruction and the constantly roving Turkish troops, who stopped any Greek they could intimidate. Aristotle managed to ingratiate himself with the Turks living in his house by supplying them with some liquor, a precious commodity in the city then that was very difficult to secure. Through friends, he managed to get a few bottles of Raki and ouzo for the Turks and for the U.S. Vice Consul, John L. Parker, an influential friend of the family who had been driving all over the countryside looking for some liquor to present to the captain of a U.S. ship sitting in the harbor. Hoping that Aristotle would continue to supply them with alcohol, the Turks rewarded him with a *laisser-passer*, complete with his photograph and fingerprints, which enabled him to move freely about the city. In addition, Parker gave Aristotle an entry pass to the U.S. Marine Zone which enclosed the partially burned American Consulate. It was a haven of safety should he ever need it. Equipped with his two safe-passage documents and dressed in a new suit which he had planned to wear to Oxford, Aristotle, looking and acting somewhat like a young diplomat, quickly went about the business of taking care of his family. He visited his father in prison and discovered to his horror that each night Greeks by the scores were being given kangaroo military trials. Inevitably, all were found guilty and executed on the spot. There was every reason to believe that if he remained in prison long enough, Socrates, too, would be hung.

Aristotle went to all of his father's Turkish friends and business associates and told them of his father's plight. He didn't have to persuade them to sympathize with him. They were all—almost to a man—incensed, since in many cases Socrates had put them in business, extended credit lines, and kept them going for years when times were difficult. A protest was planned while Aristotle attempted to locate the rest of his family. His mother and sisters, he learned, had been shipped to the island of Lesbos to await evacuation to Greece, but he could find no record or information about his grandmother.

Depressed, but determined to carry on, he made an official request, which was granted, to visit the totally burned out section of the city where his father's offices had been located. The area was cordoned off. Not all of the dead had been cleared out and the smell of burning flesh still pervaded the air. In Socrates' office, there were several safes containing Turkish pounds. Aristotle's father had given him the combinations in case they had survived the fire and been overlooked by the looters. Accompanied by several soldiers, Aristotle worked and dug through the ruins and eventually located two of the safes. Inside one they found several thousand Turkish pounds, the equivalent of $4,000 or $5,000.

Although Socrates had several bank accounts in Switzerland, England and other countries, it was impossible for him, working from within the prison, even with Aristotle outside, to get a transfer of funds within a reasonably short time. In any event, most bank accounts were frozen, and if outside money had reached Smyrna it would most likely have been confiscated by the Turks. Yet if he didn't get a sizable amount of cash quickly, Socrates' chances for survival were very slim. The prison guards provided edible food only if they were paid well for it. They were also willing to keep Socrates' name off each day's execution roster—for a price. Without money, any day could be Socrates' last.

Aristotle's attempts to inspire Socrates' friends were successful. A band of about fifty Turkish businessmen led by Aristotle marched to the prison and picketed on Socrates' behalf. When the head of the prison met with some of the organizers of the demonstration, he was told that if it hadn't been for Socrates' philanthropy and trust, many a Turkish Smyrnan would have starved to death or at least have been counted among the poor.

The protest worked. Although he was not released, Socrates was moved to another part of the prison, away from the Greeks who were ultimately condemned to die, and told that there was a possibility that he might be set free. Aristotle secretly gave his father several hundred pounds so that the guards could be bribed to offer better food, tobacco and other amenities. Socrates' life seemed assured, for a while, though Aristotle was still unsure of exactly how to extricate him.

He was also terribly worried about how the rest of his family, without money, was coping in Greece. To complicate matters, the Turkish government had established a new law by which all Greek males between the ages of 17 and 45 either had to leave the country or face an indeterminate sentence in a concentration camp. Since he was nearing the dangerous age, Aristotle had to make fast plans for his own emigration.

Socrates urged his son to leave Smyrna and to locate and settle the family in Athens. He was certain of his eventual release through the help of his Turkish friends and was concerned about the well-being of his mother, wife and daughters.

There is a story, confirmed by Onassis, that on the day that he last visited the prison, the warden detained and questioned him about the amount of money he had given his father and about the family's relationship to the Greek government. He was threatened with torture and solitary confinement if he refused to cooperate. Just then, the phone rang. Called to an emergency meeting, the warden left the young boy in his office under guard. Aristotle escaped when the guard was paying attention to something else, and since he had walked freely through the prison gates for weeks, he was not stopped as he left the grounds. Once outside, he ran the three-mile distance to the U.S. Marine Zone, "like a leopard," as he recalled it, and was hidden there by Vice-Consul Parker until he could be placed on an American destroyer heading for Greece.

20

However he actually traveled to Greece, when he arrived he located his family, who were staying with distant cousins, and there was a tearful reunion. Counting his immediate family and all the aunts, uncles and cousins, there were almost two dozen members of the family living together in substandard conditions. It was up to Aristotle, who had his father's money to use and safeguard, to provide for this extended family. From all of the Onassis' holdings, there was approximately $100,000, but it had to be shared among a number of relatives — including Aristotle's mother and father, their four children, their four sisters-in-law, seven nieces and nephews. The major portion of Socrates' fortune, the money that he had in Turkish banks in Smyrna, could not be withdrawn and all of that — several hundred thousand dollars — was eventually lost.

Unfortunately, one member of the family was missing — Gethsemane, his grandmother. Eventually, the pitiful story was revealed to Aristotle. Although separated in Turkey from her daughter-in-law and grandchildren, the old lady survived the hardships and indignities of the Turks and made her way from an evacuation camp on the island of Samos to the Athens port of Piraeus, only to be attacked, ironically, by a group of Greek thieves. Badly beaten and in shock, she died the day after the assault. Aristotle was heartbroken over her death, and for a while paid a daily visit to the cemetery, in Piraeus, where she was buried.

At that time, Aristotle had his fortune told by a friend of the family, and years later he described the prophecy: "Western Europeans do it with tea leaves but the Greeks use coffee grounds. One prediction was that my father would be released in a few weeks. Another was that I would have a dispute and go to the ends of the earth and do well there. Finally, the coffee grounds predicted that I would not marry for a long, long time. Every bit of it came true."

Once the family was settled in a safe and reasonably comfortable house in the Kifizia section of Athens, Onassis journeyed back to Turkey by way of an Egyptian ship, in an effort to extricate his father from prison. Instead of going to Smyrna, however, he went to the seat of the Turkish government, Constantinople. Using his father's banking and tobacco contacts as intermediaries, government officials and those in charge of the penal system were approached to see what could be done. Promises were made. Money changed hands. To secure Socrates' freedom, it cost about $25,000 in bribes to the right people. Eventually, Socrates was pardoned, bought his own way on a commercial liner rather than wait, perhaps months, for official passage, and sailed for Greece.

Coincidentally, both son and father arrived in Athens at approximately the same time. Aristotle was astonished to be met by his father's displeasure and criticism. Although his father was pleased to be out of prison, he was certain that his release had been imminent and that the $25,000 spent by Onassis—a goodly portion of the family's fortune—was an irresponsible and wasteful act. Although no overt dispute occurred, the tension between father and son was intense and for a time they avoided talking to each other.

As a result, not only was Socrates angered and depressed at losing his business, his house and his money, but he seemed to be losing his son. Although they had been relatively close over the years, it was with his grandmother and his sister Artemis that Aristotle had had the closest familial relationship. As he matured into independence, he grew distant from his father. In the short while that he was in prison, Socrates felt that he held Aristotle's affection more closely than he had in years, but he also knew that this was based on the dramatic circumstances and dire predicament in which he found himself. Aristotle was bitter at what he felt was unjust criticism, and Socrates felt his son drawing still further away.

There is also the possibility, and this is pure speculation, that Socrates didn't trust his own son, believing that a great portion of the $25,000 extrication money went into a hidden bank account in Aristotle's name. It would have been a simple thing to do. All of the dealings were made in cash, naturally without receipts or documents, and for a highly ambitious young man, as Aristotle was beginning to show himself to be, the temptations might have proved irresistible.

In the weeks that followed, the rift between the two grew. Aristotle did not quite know what to do with his life.

There was constant talk and tears over what had occurred in Smyrna, "nothing else, day after day," Aristotle remembered. "I was just seventeen and seventeen just doesn't nurse its sorrows forever." He felt hurt, angry and insecure that his father believed he had made a tragic mistake with the family's savings and the idea that he might possibly have failed his father was intolerable to him. There was no longer enough money to attend Oxford, or any university for that matter, and even if there had been, it is unlikely that Socrates would have given it to his now alienated son. Although Socrates intended to begin his tobacco business in Athens, this would take time, and it was unthinkable that Aristotle would ever work for his father again.

While he was deciding what to do, Aristotle performed whatever heavy household chores were needed, and he accompanied his two sisters to school in Piraeus each day and met them afterwards to bring them home. Eventually, it became apparent that the opportunities for work or business almost anywhere in Greece were so competitive as to be impossible. The 1,500,000 newly repatriated Greeks, now crowding an already economically depressed country with a population of only 5,000,000, caused massive unemployment. There simply were no jobs, very little money to borrow to start businesses, and no opportunities for a relatively inexperienced youth such as Aristotle Onassis.

A number of the younger impoverished Greeks who had come from Turkey began emigrating to other countries. Buenos Aires, Argentina, half a world away, was rich and cosmopolitan, and its growth offered many opportunities; immigration restrictions were few and comparatively easy to overcome, thus, it was experiencing a massive influx of Greek immigrants. Some of Aristotle's friends and a few distant relatives were already there. Although the possibilities were unknown, and he spoke no Spanish, Aristotle believed it might be a place to start his career. He had been in Athens just a few weeks, but he felt he had to leave Greece because of his father and because of the impossibility of making any money. "There simply weren't enough dollars to go around. I was young and strong and able to make my own way so why should I freeload any longer?" he had asked. He was also embittered, still humiliated from his father's criticism and determined to make a success of himself. He borrowed enough money from his family for a one-way ticket to Buenos Aires. Socrates also gave him $100 in cash. Although he offered his son more, Aristotle took only what he thought he would need to get to South America.

On August 3, 1923, Aristotle, accompanied by his sisters and a few other relatives, took a streetcar to the docks of Piraeus and there said his good-byes and boarded an overnight ferryboat to Brindisi, Italy. He was not yet 18 years old.

Late at night, the 12,000-ton *Tommaso Di Savoia*, steaming toward South America, lurched and then dropped deeply into the next high wave, one of a series that had been, for hours, churning up the storm-tossed and blackened waters of the South Atlantic.

Below decks, in steerage, more than 1,000 Italian and Greek immigrants lay on the pipes and on large packs of dunnage—wooden piles—upon which they had constructed small pallets to sleep. Although there were small bathrooms below, there were no showers or bathing facilities, nor any ventilation, and the smell of vomit and unwashed bodies was overwhelming. People reeled and fell; some were hurt quite seriously. Sleep, of course, was impossible. Jammed together, most of them were exhausted and sick; some lay with their eyes tightly closed, trying to block out the noises, the stench, and the jarring motion as they fought to control their heaving stomachs. Others held each other in the pitch darkness, moaning and crying as the ship rose and fell, again and again, all night long.

By early morning, the sea was calm. Onassis forced himself to his feet and stumbled to the entranceway to the stairs, bribed his way through the guards to the deck of the ship and was greeted by the rising sun and a crisp, bright morning.

He gave a few cents to a sailor who was washing the deck, stripped to his underpants and hosed himself down from head to foot. Although the water was cold and his body shivered violently, it felt magnificent to be clean and able to breathe fresh air. He vowed he would never again go below to steerage.

Even before Onassis left Athens, a feeling of excitement had begun and it raced through him when he glimpsed the ferry at Piraeus. The moment of farewell with his family at the wharf had badly depressed him, but the excitement mounted, again, as the boat pulled out of the harbor. Standing at the railing, watching the sparse lights of the city recede, Onassis was filled with an intense awareness of the moment, a self-conscious realization of his present. This awareness of himself in time and place would characterize his thinking throughout his manhood, and affect his perceptions and decisions.

The overnight trip from Piraeus, through the Ionian Sea to Italy, was delightful. Onassis had his first glimpse of the island of Corfu and fell in love with it, just from the look of its Venetian buildings and streets. He hoped that someday he would be able to go back there and explore not only that island, but all of the adjoining ones.

When he arrived in Brindisi the next afternoon, he trekked across the hot, sleepy town to the railroad station and there boarded a train to Naples. During the daylong trip, he listened alertly to the Italian language spoken around him and by the time the train reached his destination, he already knew over two dozen Italian words.

Waiting for his boat, the *Tommaso Di Savoia*, to leave for Buenos Aires, Onassis stayed in a run-down boarding house in Naples for three weeks. Most of his time was spent visiting the docks, watching the boat being loaded, and learning Italian from the shopkeepers and from his landlady's daughter. Handsome, intelligent, respectful, and able to put people at ease, Onassis charmed not only the daughter, but the landlady herself. When the time came to board the ship, the woman refused payment and both she and her daughter begged him to stay. He actually considered remaining, but he thought that the opportunities in South America were too compelling.

The voyage to South America began grimly with Aristotle sleeping in steerage, a cramped dormitory of a room in the hold of the ship. After several days of tolerating the worst of conditions — one poor meal a day, no fresh air, no proper sanitary facilities — Onassis gave the ship's purser five dollars to allow him to sleep on deck in a storage bin that held the coiled stern lines. For the remainder of the journey, he came and went as he pleased, suntanning himself by day and sleeping comfortably in the bin at night. Instead of participating in the black inferno of steerage, he made friends with the ship's Italian crew and with several of the wealthier Italian passengers, who made the crossing in relatively comfortable cabins. Onassis used his time well, deliberately determining to learn their language. Italian was, he had discovered, widely spoken in Argentina, and he wanted to have a head start over his countrymen who were in steerage.

Since he already spoke fluent Greek, Turkish and French, he found it relatively easy to absorb yet another language, and by the time the ship reached South America Onassis was tanned, rested and fluent in Italian. He sailed up the Rio de la Plata to Buenos Aires and stepped ashore on September 21, 1923, with approximately sixty dollars in his pocket.

Onassis was officially a displaced person. He had lost his Turkish citizenship when he was evacuated from Smyrna and he traveled to Argentina on a Nansen passport, a visa good for a single one-way journey from one country to another, issued by the League of Nations. He applied for Argentinian citizenship within a few weeks of stepping ashore. When he fulfilled the brief residency requirements, he was ultimately granted it.

In tracing the rise of Aristotle Onassis in the world of commerce and finance, the question usually arises as to whether he had any financial assistance from his father. In fact, he actually did begin his career, Horatio Alger-like, with that now legendary sixty dollars, all the money he had in the world. It is true that once Socrates' tobacco business began to prosper again in Greece, he was able to help his son, but Aristotle never quite forgot nor forgave his father's criticism about his release from prison, and although he did seek his father's business help, he never took nor borrowed money from him again.

Buenos Aires, the Paris of South America, with a population of over two million people, was a bustling, cosmopolitan city of outdoor cafes, small green parks, broad boulevards, and palm-shaded plazas. The vivacity of the city seemed to promise the opportunity he was seeking. Onassis was already obsessed with the idea of amassing a fortune, although his standards at that time were quite modest. Only by gaining wealth himself could he justify his judgment and prove to himself, if not to his father, that he had acted responsibly in paying so large a ransom for Socrates' freedom.

At first, he lived with one of his father's distant cousins; but the man was old, sloppy in his ways, with personal habits that the increasingly fastidious Onassis could not abide. He moved into a small boardinghouse where, for approximately seven dollars a week, he received his room and meals. The Italian that he had learned served him well as a prologue to *porteno* Spanish, which had many of the same rhythms and many similar words. Popularly called Rio Platense, it was spoken by most of the people who lived or worked near the port in the solidly Italian section *la Boca*. Within a short while, Onassis could speak passable Spanish, with the characteristic Argentinian accent that makes the language sound somewhat Gallic, rather than Latin.

But his success with the language did nothing to improve his meager finances. Onassis had begun to haunt the waterfront area, trying to find work. At first, he looked for stevedore jobs, waking early each morning, going persistently from one dock to another as the ships pulled in, joining the crowds of men and boys waiting hopefully to be allowed to do the strenuous work of unloading the heavy cargoes. Eventually, he even tried signing on as a cabin boy or engine wiper on one of the many Greek ships in the harbor. Always, he had no luck. He did make some money working at temporary jobs, which included dishwashing, bricklaying and rowing people across the Riachuelo River.

At night, the waterfront area took on the atmosphere of a carnival and Onassis would sit at an outside *trattoria*, drink a glass of inexpensive house wine, eat spaghetti with butter sauce and watch the world go by. He was lonely, but exhilarated with the visions of a new world.

Finally, he was hired to be a full-time dishwasher at a waterfront cafe. He was to begin work the next day. Wandering through the noisy streets just off the docks studded with dilapidated houses, making idle conversation with some sailors, he happened to hear of a British ship that was scheduled to leave for London in a few days. He rushed over to the pier where the ship was berthed, and signed on as a deckhand. Two jobs in one day: he was exultant. He was also wryly amused at the irony of returning to Europe after only a few weeks in South America, but he seemed to have no choice. It was certainly better than washing dishes.

Had he gone through with his plan, this would have been the only opportunity Aristotle Onassis ever had to actually work aboard a ship, even though his life would ultimately be dependent on ships. But it never happened. The next day, he met some young Greek immigrants on a streetcar. They mentioned that there was work available, even for those without experience, at the British United River Plate Telephone Company, an affiliate of International Telephone and Telegraph. Aristotle applied for a job the very next day, was hired immediately and given an intensive three-week course in the inner workings of the telephone company. All of the telephones of metropolitan Buenos Aires were being converted to an automatic dialing system and there was need for workers of all kinds and categories. Aristotle was given some preliminary training as a welder of thin telephone wires, at the rate of twenty-five cents an hour, more than enough to pay for his room and board and any other necessities.

The job proved to be a boon. Once he had become adept at the work, he was on demand to work overtime past five o'clock at the rate of time and a half his normal pay. As a result, just a few weeks after starting the job, he was making a take-home salary of over forty dollars a week which, by Argentine standards, was a great deal of money. As soon as he could afford it, he became a member of L'Aviron, a yacht and rowing club. He was still good at rowing and enjoyed it. His strong arms and broad chest grew broader with frequent practice. Outside of this relaxation, though, he was quite frugal with his money and saved as much as he could. Whenever he saw the possibility that advancement to another level in the company could earn him more money, though not necessarily prestige or status, he applied for it. Hence, he immediately accepted the chance to work as a telephone operator for special calls, at night from 7 P.M. to 7 A.M., at one of the biggest exchanges in the city. It was not a particularly strenuous job and he had the opportunity to read and even to sleep. Each time a call came in, a buzzer woke him and he put through the connection. Already his Spanish was so good that he could understand and follow complicated instructions on the phone. By constantly talking and listening to Spanish on the telephone, he continued to perfect it. Since Buenos Aires had many other nationals living there, he had the opportunity to listen to and speak other languages as well. Although he had studied some English and German in school, it was as a switchboard operator that he gained fluency in those languages.

Aristotle kept the job as nighttime switchboard operator for over six months. By working overtime, sometimes on Saturdays and Sundays, and by spending very little money, he managed to accumulate a savings of close to $1,000. The achievement of this first financial success in such a short time, based on his own industry and prudence, undoubtedly encouraged Onassis to expand his horizons.

Determined to build a business that was as successful, or more, than his father's had been in Smyrna, Aristotle
began to look into the commercial possibilities of importing
Oriental tobaccos into South America. Based on his experience
in Turkey and the knowledge he'd gained from his father, it
was a field that he felt confident with. He knew that in getting
started he would have access to his father's international
tobacco contacts, some of whom had come to know Aristotle
quite well during his father's imprisonment. They were still
in the business and could be counted on for some assistance.

Turkish tobaccos were unknown in Argentina at
that time. The Argentines used the strong black leaf from
Cuba and a small amount from the North American plantations in the South. Onassis calculated that once the Argentines
smoked the better, cheaper, lighter Turkish brands, they
would become avid purchasers, so he set himself the monu-
mental but potentially rewarding task of attempting to change
the smoking habits of an entire country. People in the larger
cities in the United States were already smoking Turkish and
other Oriental cigarettes in large quantities. It was the age of
Rudolph Valentino and anything "Egyptian" or Eastern was
considered exotic and very much in vogue. "Murads," an
enticingly different Oriental cigarette, was one of the fastest
growing brands and Americans were quickly acquiring a taste
for the exquisitely mild Turkish cigarettes.

Aristotle wrote to his father and within several weeks
received a parcel containing samples of various grades of
different tobaccos that could be purchased in quantity and
imported to South America. There were enough different
kinds of great tobaccos—from Greece, Turkey, Bulgaria and
other Balkan countries—that Aristotle was certain he would be
able to convince a cigarette manufacturer to purchase a
quantity from him. Eventually his father sent him some
samples of some of the best leaves grown in Greece and
Aristotle was now doubly convinced that, with this richly
flavored tobacco, he was destined to make a sale.

While still working at the Telephone Company at
night, Aristotle visited the tobacco companies by day, attempting to interest the chief buyers in giving him an order—even a
small one would be a beginning—for this special brand of

tobacco. Week after week went by and although every day he attempted to show and discuss his samples, he was unable to get to see someone in authority in any company who could make a decision whether to buy or not.

Eventually, he chose the one cigarette manufacturer that he believed might give him a chance. It was a firm that had experimented in the past and he was hoping that they might again. Although the buyer had already refused to see him, he stood outside the building each morning until he learned to recognize the company president, Juan Gaona. When, instinctively, he felt the time was right, Aristotle approached the man on the street just before he entered the building, and in his best Spanish explained that he had samples of some exciting new tobaccos and had been unsuccessful not only in gaining an order but even seeing anyone who could or would make a decision.

Gaona was impressed with Aristotle's sincerity and his foreigner's attempt to speak good Spanish and arranged a formal meeting for the next day with the head of the purchasing department.

After the chief buyer of the company smoked, tasted, and examined the various leaves that were offered, the man asked the price. Aristotle gave him the best and lowest price he could come up with. His idea was to establish a customer who would buy again and again once he discovered that the tobacco had gained acceptance, and he had no intention of being turned down because his price was too high. Onassis was quite willing to take a much smaller profit for himself, simply to get this initial order. The result was a sale— $10,000 worth of a Turkish leaf was bought and Aristotle Onassis was on his way to making his fortune.

During the next two years, still working at the telephone company and cautiously maintaining his inexpensive lodgings, Onassis continued to import tobaccos to Buenos Aires, where he increased the consumption of Oriental tobacco to 35 percent of the total amount used in the city. This amount came to about $2 million worth of imported leaf, with Onassis' personal profit well over $100,000.

His cousin, Constantine Konialides, son of Aristotle's

Uncle Chrysostomos who was killed in the Turkish holocaust of 1922, had also immigrated to Argentina, and the two young men decided to go into business together. With Aristotle providing the cash and Constantine the managerial time, they opened a small shop to manufacture their own luxury brands of cigarettes. At first, they employed two men who hand-rolled the cigarettes, called "Primeros" and "Osman," and wrapped them in attractive gold foil before packaging. The cigarettes were very expensive, extremely mild and tipped with rose leaves. They sold mostly to women, some of whom were taking up smoking for the first time. Claudia Muzio, the dramatic soprano and one of the great opera stars of the day, was at the height of her career when she appeared at the Colon Opera House in Buenos Aires. During her stay in the city, she was introduced to the delicate cigarettes and became fond of smoking them, even in public. For a while, possibly because of the diva's interest, Onassis' cigarettes became the rage of the female society of Buenos Aires. As the business grew, Onassis & Co. eventually had as many as 30 cigarette-makers and the demands of that business plus his constant importing of tobaccos for the larger manufacturers forced Aristotle eventually to leave his job as a switchboard operator. He later pointed out that not only did the telephone company job provide him with a base, the small amount of capital he needed to start his entrepreneurial ventures, but it also helped him to perfect his Spanish until he could speak it as well as a native.

Onassis also manufactured another brand, "Bis," which instigated the first lawsuit ever brought against him. Another cigarette maker had been manufacturing and selling "Bis" cigarettes, at the time, one of the most popular brands in Buenos Aires, before Onassis took the name for himself. The originator sued and won. Onassis was forced to pay several thousand dollars in damages, in addition to ceasing to use the name. He didn't lose money, however. By the time the court had settled the case, he had sold tens of thousands of packs of "Bis" and there were no records kept that could be subpoenaed by the court. Onassis claimed that he was unaware of the other company's use of the name.

The tobacco importing business went extremely well for Onassis. Each year he substantially increased the volume from the previous year, and it appeared as though he would become a millionaire in a relatively short amount of time if business continued as it was. But his efforts at cigarette manufacture, although they had expanded greatly from the beginning, were no longer profitable. There were hundreds of small manufacturers throughout the city, each attempting to garner the other's customers, and the competition and price cutting were fierce. Some unscrupulous businessmen were also known to use chemicals to contaminate the tobacco bales of their competitors and this kind of crime was becoming more common among the city's cigarette makers. Onassis was losing a substantial amount of money, but overall he had made a profit since the business's inception. Eventually, he decided to leave the cigarette manufacturing business as unprofitable, and to concentrate entirely on importing tobacco and other products.

To succeed in business was not all that captured the attention and ambition of Aristotle Onassis. As he began to amass wealth, he was eager to circulate in the wealthier circles of the city. He moved into a posh suite at the Plaza Hotel, ate at the best restaurants and continued to study languages. Even though he was considered somewhat rough-hewn and therefore was not totally accepted—sometimes was even ostracized—by the leaders of Argentinian society, he deliberately participated in the activities that captured the enthusiasm of the city's aristocracy.

One of these pursuits was the ballet. Although he was not particularly interested in the dance, Onassis attended from time to time for social reasons. On one particular evening he became enamored with a young Russian dancer of the Anna Pavlova Swan Ballet Company that was headlining at the Colon Opera House on one of its world tours. He claimed that he fell in love with her, just by watching her dance. Later that night, he coincidentally met the girl in the elevator of his hotel and initiated a conversation. He had dinner with her and during the course of the ballet's season dated her again and again. Eventually, he enjoyed his first true love affair with her. When the ballet company was about to return to Europe, the girl refused to go. There had been talk of marriage and although she had no intention of abandoning her career as a dancer, she was adamant about not leaving him. Onassis had a strong flavor of impending success about him that some women found intoxicating, almost aphrodisiacal.

Pavlova personally visited Onassis and urged him to talk the girl into not relinquishing her career and into continuing with the troupe. He agreed that this was sensible. He was not ready for marriage yet, nor was the girl, he believed. He attempted to persuade her to go on with Pavlova, but she refused. Before long, she became a soloist with the local ballet company. A story was circulated at that time that the girl was pregnant and years later a story—totally without substantiation—was published in a local gossip column that she gave birth, in secrecy, to a baby boy whom Onassis continued to support until he reached manhood. It is known that his affair with the ballet dancer lasted for about a year until it broke up for undisclosed reasons.

With his increasing business success, more rumors ran rampant about him. Another unsubstantiated story about Onassis' love life when in South America, which I have included here without source or belief, was that he married a wealthy Bolivian girl, who was a militant revolutionary. Although she gave Onassis some of her father's money, so the story goes, it was a minimal amount. She supposedly was killed in an uprising two years after they were wed.

Although Onassis was always ready to have a good time and spend an evening in the various night clubs around the city, it was business that consumed his true interests. He looked into all markets, constantly searching for ways to make money. In addition to his tobacco importing business which was booming, he began to import and export grains, wool, salt and hides, and he occasionally acted, usually with substantial profit, as a broker of whale oil. In all of these ventures, he made large amounts of money.

He was interested in getting into shipping, not as an importer or one who merely uses ships as he had been doing, but by owning ships and enjoying the highly profitable cargo rates. Alberto Dodero, a brilliant and rich Argentine shipowner, became a friend of Onassis and had an influence on him. Buy cheaply, keep your overhead low and sell for a profit, he continually advised his young friend. The cost of buying a ship seemed prohibitive to Onassis, however. If he invested all the money he owned into purchasing a freighter, he would have had little operating capital and if anything went wrong, he could have easily been wiped out.

At that time, he did allow himself one safe venture, however brief, in owning a ship. A small empty tanker had half sunk in Montevideo Harbor and was available for sale for a little more than it would cost to salvage her — about $10,000. Onassis first talked to the crew to determine the extent of the damage, found that the repair costs would be within reason and then, with the advice of Dodero, determined that comparable ships of the same weight, age and condition were selling for at least ten times the amount it would cost him to put this one in order. He quickly took a speedboat across the Rio de la Plata to Uruguay and negotiated the sale — in cash — with the ship's owner. Within a matter of days, the ship was afloat and thoroughly repaired, and a week later Onassis sold it, at a huge profit, to a local steamship company.

The ability to make large amounts of money came easily to Onassis, because of his early family experience in finance, a stubborn perseverance, a readiness to work at all times, an alertness born of need, a talent for manipulation, a studied courtesy, and an uncanny ability always to sense where the possibilities of making money might be. He possessed an energy, pure in form, that perpetuated and strengthened itself as he continued in business. With each success, the next step, tempered with confidence, was that much easier. Just as any master craftsman, he learned the trade, the art and the science of making money, and his development of the skill was with great precision. It became to him an ecstasy of a very real sort. He was totally conscious of his prowess and had every intention of continuing to generate it.

The year was 1929, six years since he had come to Argentina, almost penniless, to make his way in the world. He had just celebrated his 23rd birthday. His estimated worth was $1 million.

4

Onassis had spent the hot Athens morning sitting patiently in the sweltering anteroom of the office of the Minister of Foreign Affairs. A propellor-like ceiling fan rotated slowly and seemed to generate little or no wind. On one wall was an excellent portrait in oil of Eleutherios Venizelos; on another, a large framed photograph of the Acropolis—wastefully redundant since it was possible to see the real Parthenon from the office window ablaze in the morning light. He had been in the office since 10 A.M. and now it was approaching lunch time. "I'm sorry, Mr. Onassis, will you please return at 5 P.M.," said a thin, officious aide suddenly appearing from the inner office. "Mr. Michalakopoulos has been called to a special cabinet meeting and cannot see you right now."

Onassis had a slow, heavy lunch in a small downstairs restaurant on Academious Street and then dreamed and calculated away the afternoon as he sat sipping tonic under a palm tree in an outdoor cafe in Syntagma Square, not far from the Minister's office. After almost a dozen letters requesting an appointment with the proper government official, he had been finally granted an audience. He had waited two years for this day and as humiliated and annoyed as he was to have been kept waiting, he attempted to maintain his composure. His livelihood depended on the result of his meeting with Michalakopoulos. Over and over again, he rehearsed his arguments and rationales as his thoughts competed with the noise of the afternoon traffic.

In the summer of 1929, after six years away from his family, Onassis decided to pay a visit to Greece. His father was ill, and there was still some enmity between them, but the bitterness had been somewhat dispelled as they worked together, via cables and the mail, in building Aristotle's tobacco import business. Without his father to provide him the best of samples and to aid him in the actual purchase and shipping of the tobacco to Argentina, Onassis might not have grown as quickly and as successfully as he had. It is also true that Socrates had profited and his own business was bolstered by the tens of millions of dollars of Turkish tobaccos that his son had bought and shipped to Argentina. Aristotle was already much wealthier than his father had ever been and Socrates may have had a paradoxical feeling of hidden resentment and overt pride at his son's accomplishments.

Aristotle had been sending home money not only to his immediate family but to all of his widowed aunts and other relatives who had never recovered their losses from the 1922 purge. He had become the head of the family. Onassis once remarked, "By then they were asking me, *from Athens*, who should marry whom and where the boys should go to school. For my father to have lived long enough to see that has given me more satisfaction than any other achievement in my whole life."

It is not difficult to imagine the family's reaction to

38

the confident, prodigal son, now a millionaire and traveling first class, alighting on the same dock at Piraeus from which he had departed as a humiliated and embittered young man six years before.

Onassis returned to Athens to see his family again, and also because he had legitimate business interests that were calling him back. Difficulties with a trade treaty between Greece and Bulgaria had been smoldering for quite awhile and the tangential repercussions were greatly interfering with Onassis' profit. Greece had initiated a decree that sharply increased the import tax on any goods from countries with which it did not have a signed treaty. Argentina was one of those countries. In retaliation against the Greek tax, it raised its import tax to such an exorbitant extent that Onassis might have been driven out of business if the situation had continued, since it was difficult to pay such a tax on the prevailing rate of tobacco and still make a profit. Not only was his business at stake, but almost 80 percent of the Greek merchant fleet would have had to cease functioning, since as callers on the port of Buenos Aires with cargoes of grain, coal, tobacco and other goods, they would have been taxed out of profitable existence. If he could convince Greek authorities to discontinue the levy on Argentinian ships, Argentina would undoubtedly reciprocate. Onassis wrote letters to everyone in the Greek government that he knew but as month after month went by with hardly a reply, let alone any positive action, he prepared a carefully researched and well-reasoned memorandum outlining the role that the Greek shipping fleet played in helping the entire Greek economy, especially as it related to shipments of goods to Argentina.

Even though he received some favorable comments by mail from Greek governmental officials about the logic of his thesis, still nothing was done. It was then that he decided that a trip to Greece would be necessary. Once there, he hoped he could arrange a face-to-face meeting with officials of either the Bureau of Foreign Affairs or the Maritime Commission, which would have the power to bring about the effect he was seeking. After several days of family dinners and parties celebrating his return, Socrates arranged a meeting between his son and the legendary Premier of Greece, Eleutherios Venizelos, who probably consented to the audience because of the financial and moral support that Socrates had given him over the years.

Venizelos was impressed enough with the intelligence, vitality and logic of Onassis that he sent the memorandum to Andreus Michalakopoulos, his Minister of Foreign Affairs, with a note telling him to study it and to meet with its originator as soon as possible. Even with this impetus from the Premier, it took Onassis almost two weeks before he sat in the office, facing the man he so desperately wanted to see. As Onassis enthusiastically explained his position and elaborated on his report, Michalakopoulos acted as if he weren't listening. Rudely filing his nails, he appeared to be somewhat bored by the conversation. It became obvious to Aristotle that he had been granted the meeting with Michalakopoulos, only because the Premier had instructed that it should happen, perhaps from courtesy rather than need or diligence. Many years later, Onassis related the dialogue that took place, "The Minister finally told me 'I like your report, young man, but I am very busy. Do give your name and telephone number to my secretary on your way out. I will think about it and shall write and keep in touch, Mister . . . Mister . . . Anisos . . . .' I was furious and told him that I could see how busy he was. As I stood in front of his desk, I said, 'I had hoped you would give some practical consideration to a very desperate situation, but you really haven't listened to anything I've talked about. You're more interested in your nails than in Greek commerce.'"

As Onassis abruptly turned to leave, Michalakopoulos, realizing his mistake and intrigued by the strength of personality of the young man before him, was on his feet in a second, apologizing and letting him know that he *had* listened to everything that Onassis had said, and that, indeed, something would be done about the situation. He then insisted that Onassis be seated again, offered him a cigar and began exploring his background.

Several days later, Aristotle received a call from the Bureau of Foreign Affairs. It was the assistant who had shown him out that first morning, saying that Michalakopoulos would like another meeting with him. After checking his credentials and receiving some value judgments on the young man's capabilities and character, Michalakopoulos was convinced that, despite Onassis' youth and relative inexperience, he would be the perfect liaison for Greece with the Argentine government in an attempt to negotiate a trade agreement. Although he had been back in Athens just about two weeks, Aristotle Onassis was soon sailing to Argentina with diplomatic status, as Envoy Extraordinary of Greece. It was just a matter of a few visits to the proper Argentine officials before serious negotiations were begun between the two countries. Soon, a reciprocally advantageous trade agreement between Argentina and Greece was reached.

As a result of his success, Onassis was appointed in December 1929 Greek Consul General in Buenos Aires.

Onassis soon discovered that his new government job and the operation of his tobacco business gave him little time to sleep. The Buenos Aires harbor was accommodating over one thousand Greek ships a year, better than three a day, and with each ship he had to find time to organize his consulate staff to complete the paperwork, which he had to approve, while also settling disputes and strikes. Negotiating the complicated legal problems connected with international trade often kept him at the office until late at night. However, the most important positive factor was that he thoroughly learned the machinations of the shipping industry, as the post of consul proved to be a business listening-post of incalculable value. He was constantly visiting and inspecting ships, talking to shipowners and other importers and quietly absorbing everything, making a very conscious attempt to learn as much as he could before going into shipowning seriously. The dream of owning and operating ships was foremost in his mind, and like all good businessmen, he was determined to know everything about his subject before investing a penny.

Onassis befriended a young man, a fellow Greek named Costa Gratsos, who knew a great deal about the sea and ships. He had been an apprentice seaman and was a member of a well-known Greek family, the Dracoulis, famous for their ships. Gratsos advised Aristotle on everything he knew about maritime law and the general operation of not only a single ship but of a fleet, and the two men became best friends. In addition to business, they shared what would become an insatiable desire for nightclubbing and the pursuit of attractive women.

Apparently Onassis felt no dichotomy in his life-style. As Consul General he was invited to state dinners and elaborate political banquets of the upper crust and he always attended — but not without a certain feeling of uneasiness that he might be out of his element. His motivation in appearing at these functions was to make contacts and circulate among the great and near-great, an endeavor which he felt might help him to further his career. His carousing was on a different level; but it was an activity he would pursue slavishly, leaving the ballet or opera to spend the remainder of the evening at clubs that were barely more than striptease "joints." One crucial factor that was at least partially responsible for his evening activities was he needed very little sleep. Since his early childhood, all he ever required were 3 or 4 hours of sleep each night and he was known to be able to work 48, even 72 hours at a time without any sleep at all, then collapsing into bed and sleeping 12 or 14 hours, awaking totally refreshed. Insomnia was not his problem. His avoidance of sleep was a studied and tutored habit. "Why waste your life sleeping?" he once asked. "I don't have time for it!"

Onassis continuously looked for opportunities to become a shipowner and operator, and as his tobacco importing business continued to grow, he traveled to London, Amsterdam, Antwerp and the other great ports of the world, and to the shipyards of many countries, looking for, and learning about ships.

In the winter of 1931, he opened a small office in London, partly to aid his tobacco business but mainly to serve as the base of operations for what he felt would be the beginning of a career as a serious shipowner. It was at this time that he finally stumbled on what he was seeking and characteristically he realized that the propitious time had come. He heard that the Canadian National Steamship Company had a small fleet of freighters docked at Montreal for two years which they were putting up for sale. Facing bankruptcy, they had little choice but to take just a fraction of the value of the ships which had originally cost about $2 million each. At 8,500 to 10,000 tons each, and only ten to twelve years old, comparable ships were selling for about $100,000 at the time, but the great depression adversely affected every industry. Shipping was especially suffering. There were many ships, but no cargoes.

As soon as Onassis heard they were for sale, he was in Montreal to see the ships. Although they were beginning to rust, the ships were basically in excellent condition and could be put into floating operation with only a small expenditure. Onassis trudged up and down the snowcovered decks, and accompanied by a small personal entourage of local engineers whom he had hired especially to aid him, he minutely inspected the boiler rooms and inner workings of each ship. After several days of looking at all ten ships, he decided that there were six in which he was definitely interested.

Onassis had long since begun to formulate a personal business philosophy, which evolved out of his experiences as a boy making deliveries for his father in Smyrna. He learned from his success in dealing with the Turks during their occupation of his home and their imprisonment of his father. It took form as he began to develop his own businesses in Buenos Aires, was strengthened with his successes persuading Venizelos and Michalakopoulos to reconsider the import tax, and was nurtured as he gained negotiating skills as the Greek Consul General. Now he could see it clearly: The key to success was boldness, boldness, and more boldness. This seemed an excellent time to put the theory to the test.

Without hesitation, Onassis made an offer of $20,000 per ship, as he described it, "The price of a single Rolls Royce." This was approximately the amount of money the owners could have realized if they had sold the ships for scrap metal. The offer was almost insultingly low, but Onassis had concluded that because the ships had been docked for two years, the steamship company had apparently been unable to sell them. He chose to gamble on the possibility that he was the only bidder. He had also determined the scrap metal price for each vessel, assuming that the company, because of its desperate position, might have

43

also priced those figures in case it could not find a buyer for the ships. Onassis' next step was purely psychological — he reasoned that if the company needed the cash quickly, as it did, then in order to save face it would be more inclined to sell the ships to a new owner and keep them afloat, rather than see them relegated to a junk heap.

He had the disconcerting habit of talking in spurts and laughing very loud at moments when one would think it was time to be quiet. It kept the shipowners off balance, never quite knowing where they stood with him. As it developed, all of his conclusions and mannerisms proved correct. His offer was accepted, the sale consummated, and Aristotle Onassis was the owner of his first fleet of ships.

Onassis knew that until he could sell his first cargo, he would have to keep the boats idle, an expensive proposition in terms of docking fees and insurance, but he was confident that in a short while, he would have all of his ships at sea. Because of the continuing economic blight all over the world, however, the ships were inactive much longer than he had hoped, and he began to doubt the sagacity of his purchase.

It took almost two years before Onassis secured the first cargo for one of his ships, a consignment of newsprint for the London *Daily Mail* paper. It was the first and only time he would ever carry bulk paper on one of his ships, but it was a profitable shipment and gave him a key push to extricating his ships from their docks.

Since the economy showed little promise of reversing itself, Onassis was forced to sell four of the freighters, at a profit; he did have enough shipping business to keep the remaining two on the seas almost constantly. Eventually, the two ships would be working steadily and bringing in large profits — the great Onassis fortune was becoming a reality.

Onassis spent almost all of his time working. He would pore over shipping journals from Antwerp, Vancouver, Hamburg and New York, looking for intelligence, trends, opportunities. He would scan, study and memorize tonnage, prices, insurance rates and schedules of the world's great and small steamship companies and then attempt to outbid his competitors. He read the maritime sections of at least six foreign language daily newspapers each day and was always *au courant* as to what cargoes were selling for and what trends would most likely begin at almost any port in the world. He began to travel voraciously—at first, to save time, on the German airship the *Graf Zeppelin*, which had initiated an inexpensive run from Argentina to Europe, and later on other airlines as their coverage of the world became more extensive. Onassis loved dirigibles. With their plush staterooms, grand salons and first-class dining service, they attempted to rival the great passenger ships. He considered booking passage on the *Hindenburg* for her much publicized maiden flight in 1937, but business needs prevented it. Shocked by her tragic crash, he abandoned flying for several years, resorting to travel by train, ship and wherever possible and practical by driving—he thought nothing of driving halfway across Europe or from Paris to Stockholm, for example, rarely stopping until he reached his destination. Whenever he traveled by ship, he used the time aboard to learn. He was always in the ship's engine room and often, after making friends with a ship's officer, on the bridge itself, keeping alert to all of the complexities that keep a ship afloat. His cousin Constantine Konialides ran the shipping office in Buenos Aires when Onassis was away on business trips.

At first, all of Onassis' ships were registered under either Greek or Argentine flags, but he soon learned that there were great advantages to be had by registering them elsewhere, even though it might be considered as somewhat unethical. Greek registration was particularly offensive to Onassis. General Metaxas, the Greek dictator, attempted to gain the support of labor by instituting welfare funds, minimum wage laws and a series of maritime laws and regulations (such as featherbedding and compulsory hiring from a rotation list) which made it difficult, by Onassis' standards, to make a profit sailing a ship under a Greek flag. And so, in addition to securing profitable cargoes for his ships, Onassis began a practice of registering them under a so-called "flag of convenience." This guaranteed that he would have to pay little or no taxes for any profits he made from those ships, and it saved him money by lowering wages for the crews and by reducing

45

safety standards. The result, to him, was the realization of even greater profits.

Onassis applied to Panama to register one of his ships, and it was accepted. The fee to establish a shipping corporation in Panama was less than $500. A small country with a population of only 800,000 at that time, Panama had no major ships of its own sailing the oceans of the world. It had no corporation tax, and its individual income tax did not apply to non-resident foreign operators of ships registered under its flag. Panama's tonnage taxes were among the lowest in the world — ten cents per year per deadweight ton. If all of these money-saving dodges were not enough to convince Onassis to register his ships with Panama, the fact that no seaman's unions existed there was perhaps the most convincing factor. Without a union, he could pay his sailors minimal wages, and they would have no recourse to negotiation or argument. In the final analysis, from the very start of his career in shipping, Onassis operated his ships at approximately half the expense of his competitors, which were mainly the Swedish or English companies that dominated the entire shipping industry.

Since his expenses were, if not minimal, certainly not ruinous, Onassis could afford to quote lower prices for transporting goods by sea — in some cases much lower than the "standard" prices — and while there were a few companies who refused to deal with maverick shippers who operated under flags of convenience, there were many more who welcomed the opportunity of operating their businesses at a saving. As a result Onassis never lacked customers and his shipping business boomed. Onassis felt no pangs of conscience in sailing his ships under flags of convenience, and became indignant at the charge that his internationalism was cynical. He described it this way, "As a Greek, I belong to the West. As a shipowner, I belong to capitalism. Business objectives dictate the details of my operations. My favorite country is the one that grants maximum immunity from taxes, trade restrictions and unreasonable regulations. It is under that country's flag that I prefer to concentrate my profitable activities. I call this 'business sense.'" He also registered some of his ships with Liberia, and the system of securing registry papers for conven-

46

ience spread to other shipowners. As a result, Liberia's annual tonnage went from zero in 1939 to 25 million two decades later, making it one of the largest shipping nations in the world.

Although his freighters were making enormous profits, Onassis continually thought of the future. With a prescience that was uncanny, similar to his instinct that Argentina was ready for Oriental tobacco, he saw the possibilities of the growing consumption of oil due to the world-wide adoption of motors. He concluded that coal would eventually be replaced as a source of power by oil in almost every corner of the globe and that supertankers, huge warehouses afloat, were going to become the most economical way to transport what was destined to be among the most valuable cargoes ever shipped anywhere — the substance that some shippers would refer to as black gold.

Corsica was hardly discernible in the pitch of night. The only signs of life were a few lights sparking the town of Ajaccio, the birthplace of Napoleon, or an occasional mountaintop campfire. The *Augustus* steamed past the island into the blackness of the Ligurian Sea. By dawn, it would reach Genoa. Some of the Genovese sailors were already celebrating being in their beautiful city. They called it *La Superba*.

Onassis was tense because he felt he was losing. The negotiation was more difficult and complex than any of his business deals. For over a week, he had been attempting to convince Ingebord Dedichen to drive to Venice with him when the boat docked at Genoa. The implication was clear. If she accepted his invitation, she would have to eventually become his mistress. He was fascinated by her; she wasn't sure what she wanted. Her friends aboard ship kept asking about "that dark little man who keeps following you around." He had barely taken his eyes off the tall, willowy Norwegian from the moment she boarded the *Augustus*. At Buenos Aires, when she stepped up the gangplank with a bouquet of red roses in her hands, Onassis *knew*.

"Venice is the most romantic city in the world. I feel it is *my* city," he told her. They spoke in English. "It is only right that we begin there." She parried, "Begin what? I have friends expecting me in Monte Carlo. Venice is over 250 kilometers from Genoa. It would take *days* from my schedule."

Onassis looked at her with what she would later describe as "dark, somber, unforgettable eyes" and appeared to be beaten. He then tried talking to her in Swedish, using the few words he had learned from one of his *concierges* in Buenos Aires. She smiled broadly at his attempt to please her.

"You must go with me," he said with his eyes, his hands. "You will go with me. There can be no other way."

In 1934, on a leisurely business trip to Europe, Onassis traveled aboard the packet steamer *Augustus* from Buenos Aires to Genoa. On the first night out to sea, sitting in the small cocktail lounge for first-class passengers, he became intrigued by a group of Scandinavians who were traveling together. All were tall, attractive, well-dressed, heavily-tanned and talked in a polyglot of languages. He would learn later that they spoke fifteen languages among them. These sophisticates were the aristocracy of Norwegian shipping and had just returned from a scientific expedition to Antarctica. Having rested in Argentina for a week after their journey, they boarded the *Augustus* in Buenos Aires. The party included the owner of a mammoth whaling fleet, Lars Christensen, his wife, Inge, several of their friends and business associates, and one engaging young lady who particularly caught and kept Onassis' attention. She was, he thought at the time, one of the most beautiful women he had ever seen—crystal blue eyes, high cheek bones, hair so blonde it was almost white, an exquisite figure. She was always the epicenter of the group and her vivacity and elegance seemed to charm everyone. Onassis studied her from afar. He began to dream of her at night.

As the days passed aboard the ship — it took two weeks to cross the Atlantic — Onassis continually observed this young Norwegian, who he learned was named Ingebord Dedichen. He also discovered that she and her husband, international bridge player Herman Dedichen, were in the process of divorce proceedings. In the several years that they had been married, her inheritance had been depleted.

Onassis waited until the time was right to approach her. He was determined to make her acquaintance. Since he was traveling alone, the longer the journey took, the lonelier he became, and the more convinced that he was in love with her, although they had not exchanged as much as a word.

After the first day, Ingebord and her friends became aware that Onassis was staring at her in the dining room, while she was resting on deck or sitting in the lounge at night. They saw him as a strange and mysterious Levantine who drank only water or an occasional glass of wine at dinner, and speculated about his possible origins and profession — unaware, of course, that he was already a multimillionaire, and a sophisticated traveler himself.

Onassis was an expert and avid swimmer, and he would visit the ship's pool at least every morning and afternoon. One day, dressed in an old-fashioned black bathing suit with straps and chest covering, he arrived at the pool while Ingebord was teaching the Australian crawl to a fellow passenger. "That is not how it is done," barked Onassis in slightly accented French. He then dove in, swam the length of the pool and back again in perfect form, climbed out and walked away.

As the days went by, they continued to meet by accident — or by Onassis' design, in instances he carefully arranged to appear spontaneous — and ultimately developed a rapport, partially based on a mutual attraction but, at first, mainly animated by Onassis. Mostly, they strolled the upper deck of the boat, often when it was wrapped in moonlight, and talked about their lives. They both became even more interested in each other. When they learned of their mutual love and financial interest in ships, Ingebord introduced Onassis to her group, and everyone was rather surprised to find that they had some rather important common interests. Ingebord's traveling companion Lars Christensen was one of the leading shipowners in Scandinavia. After the two men got to know one another, they talked endlessly about ships. Onassis had visited Gotaverken, Sweden's largest shipyard, located in Goteborg, and had been enormously impressed with the efficient construction of the ships and the way they were financed. Scandinavian shipowners had ships built to order with a 10 percent down payment and financed the balance at a low interest which was paid over a ten-year period. This method of acquiring new ships seemed eminently more sensible and profitable to Onassis then purchasing second-hand vessels and paying full cash for them. As Onassis continued to gather information from Christensen on Scandinavian shipbuilding and financing, he learned more about and continued to pursue Ingebord.

Ingebord's father, Ingevald Bryed, a direct descendant of the Vikings, had been a multimillionaire shipowner — the most successful in Scandinavia. He was the first owner of steamships in Norway and owned the largest whaler in the world. Ingebord grew up on and around her father's ships and was the first woman in history actually to hunt whales. But Ingebord's talents were not all connected with the sea. She spent her early life at the sumptuous family castle on the southwest coast of Norway where she became expert as a horseback rider, skier, tennis player and pianist, and was accomplished in German *lieder*. Educated at the best schools in Norway and Switzerland, she was fluent in about ten languages, and she had the manners and elegance of royalty. Her parents had been the richest family in Norway and had habitually entertained statesmen and artists from around the world. Ingebord and her family had often been received at the Royal Palace and while the Bryeds were untitled, most of their friends were.

Onassis had come from a wealthy family and was already rich himself, but his money, background and bearing had the posture and sense of the Turkish docks, the gracelessness of an Oriental merchant who cozened his way to the top, rather than the more graceful and classical European refinement found in Ingebord and her family of little kings. They were an unusual pair—she, 35, formerly rich but now almost penniless, magnificently educated and self-assured, one of the most beautiful and gracious women of Norway, who had become known in many of the circles of royal and international society throughout the world; he, 28, a multimillionaire, darkly handsome, but short of stature with a heavy head, barrel chest, and extremely muscular shoulders, uncommonly reserved for a Greek, but unschooled in the etiquette of the genteel, sly, furtive, almost frightening in demeanor.

Ingebord's friends and colleagues were horrified that she would consent to spend time with Onassis, but as she described it, there really was no alternative for her, "We had an instant affinity for each other. Although he was not in the least what you could call 'well-bred,' you could sense his acute intelligence behind those dark, impish eyes, and when he smiled, he could charm mountains! He was all at once funny, tender and brutal, and his voice, his warm, sweet voice, ironic and tender, was as expressive as his southern hands, always arguing in counterpoint to his conversation. He had great magnetism."

Each time they met, they became more relaxed toward each other, and by the time they had reached Genoa, he had already proposed marriage, which she had delicately refused. He did persuade her to accompany him to Venice though; they took adjoining rooms at the deluxe Hotel Royal Daneli—perhaps the city's finest—and enjoyed an idyllic interlude, sailing on the sleepy canals, dining in the best restaurants, avoiding the museums that Onassis didn't like, and growing closer. Therein was consummated a relationship that lasted more than a dozen years and in many ways proved to be one of the most significant in Onassis' life.

After Venice, Onassis established an apartment in Paris and Ingebord spent more time there than she did in Norway, acting as the hostess of Onassis' house, decorating it, arranging dinner parties, accompanying him everywhere. The penthouse apartment at 88 Avenue Foch was in an area known as a haven for the wealthy. The building was originally owned by the late Louis Renault, the automobile manufacturer. Onassis' apartment consisted of fourteen rooms and a huge wrap-around terrace. Upon moving in, he thought the master bathroom was too small and consequently had an adjoining bedroom converted — at a cost of $75,000 — to a luxurious bathroom with a sunken rose-marble tub. Ingebord decorated the entire apartment in white and blue, and added Louis XV furniture. Ingebord introduced him to the Riviera and to Monte Carlo where they spent long weekends waterskiing, bicycling and generally leading a life of extravagant indulgence. He even talked about buying a house somewhere on the Riviera but after he priced a few, he decided against the idea. He was still paying for his Paris apartment. In a quaint and romantic way, his *sobriquet* for her was "Mamita" and hers for him was "Mamico." She once told society columnist Lloyd Shearer, "He was very unsure* of himself socially. His manners were not the best. He knew little about food, wines, clothes, culture, but he was industrious and intelligent and he learned fast." She helped in every way that she could to polish his somewhat crude and slipshod manners and mannerisms and was highly instrumental in helping him to become a diplomatic and cultivated shipping tycoon. For instance, his first dinner at the world's most renowned restaurant, Maxim's, in Paris, was with Ingebord, who carefully instructed him step-by-step on which wines to order, how to summon a waiter, and how much to tip. They visited galleries and museums together and he began to learn about great art. Before long, he was purchasing some great paintings for himself. Her schooling of Onassis continued for years, and although they were extremely, intimately in love, they were a study of the attraction of opposites. Why they never married has never been quite clear. Once, when discussing Onassis with his sister Artemis, who heartily endorsed the potential marriage of the couple, Ingebord said quixotically, "We can never marry; we're too different," and although they were opposites, it doesn't explain how the couple could manage to live together, apparently with some success, for so many years.

Onassis not only benefited from Ingebord's cultural

tutelage and hints about how to be accepted as a bona fide member of international society, but he also gained another push in his financial career as a result of his relationship with her. Although her father was dead by the time she met Onassis, it was through Ingebord's contacts that Onassis made important Scandinavian connections that eventually enabled him to get involved with the shipping interests in that area of the world.

By correspondence, he had been attempting to get Ernst Heden, the manager of the Gotaverken shipyards, interested in working with him in building a ship on terms that Onassis deemed favorable. Now, with the entree and endorsement afforded him by the names of Dedichen and Christensen, he traveled to Sweden and, unannounced, burst into Heden's office. "I had received mail from him from London, Paris, Athens and Buenos Aires," said Heden describing their meeting, "so, when my secretary said, 'Mr. Onassis wants to speak to you,' I said 'Put him through,' thinking he was on the phone. The next moment I looked up and Onassis was standing in front of my desk. In a matter of seconds, he was able to convince me to accept the deal I had refused so many times. He was a sorcerer."

He formed a new corporation, "A. S. Onassis, Goteborg, Ltd." and placed an order for a 15,000-ton oil tanker to be constructed at the gigantic Gotaverken shipyards. It was to be one of the largest tankers ever built. The average size of a tanker, then, was about 9,000 tons, and even 12,000-ton tankers were considered enormous. When Onassis' ship was completed, he christened it with the distinguished name *Ariston*. Onassis, thus, became the first Greek shipowner to own an oil tanker.

Onassis' order for such a gigantic tanker was placed because he believed in the future of the oil business and could envision enormous profits in the budding new industry. Coal was still supplying 75 percent of the world's energy. Within ten years, oil consumption would be on a rapid increase and within two decades oil would be supplying more than one-third of the world's energy. During all this time, Onassis would be in the forefront as one of the leading transporters of oil throughout the world. Oil tankers could be serviced in a fraction of the time that was needed to load a dry cargo freighter since all it took was a sophisticated pipeline connection. In addition to the great savings in wages, with a minimum of stevedores to oversee the project, there was also the safety in not being detained by the costly and constant longshoremen strikes that were common in ports all over the world. At that time, Onassis' supertankers were the largest ships of any kind in history.

While becoming involved in the construction of the *Ariston*, Onassis met Anders Jahre, a Norwegian whaling operator, who had just purchased an old U. S. Navy collier, which had carried coal for over thirty years, and although in poor shape, was still seaworthy. Jahre had paid an exorbitant price for the ship, and almost as much in refurbishing and repairing it, because he wanted a U. S. registered vessel to hunt in American waters and couldn't wait until a new ship was built for him. Onassis, who was intrigued with the whaling business, talked Jahre into allowing him to participate in the ship's ownership, and hence became involved, although on a very small scale at first, with another form of the commercial use of ships.

After construction of the *Ariston*, which cost $700,000, had been started, Onassis placed orders for two additional supertankers, the *Aristophanes*, at a $20,000 additional cost, and the *Buenos Aires* at a $40,000 increase; only 25 percent of the money having to be paid in cash during the building of the ships, the remainder being financed over a period of ten years. In addition to their size, Onassis had sumptuous owner's and crew's quarters installed in his ships, unprecedented for a ship of that type. Ingebord Dedichen designed the sitting room and two enormous bedrooms of the *Ariston* and the private accommodations included a large bath, a bar and even a grand piano.

Onassis was now certain that his ships would not only be the largest and most modern in the world, with the ability to carry as much as twice the tonnage as many of his competitors, but operating under his highly economical flags of convenience, he believed they would be among the most profitable ships afloat.

55

He continually appeared at the shipyard to check and inspect the progress of his tankers. Often he would arrive at night, after all the workers had gone home, and he would have a watchman open the gate to allow him in. He would then circle the ship again and again, climb aboard it, spend hours making mental notes of what he liked and disliked about the construction. He was quite observant about what, to others, were trifles but, to him, were important details. The next day he would call the foreman, who was always amazed that Onassis seemed to know more about the particulars of what remained to be finished than he did, and comment, complain and make suggestions about the work. He often quoted Napoleon: *"Le culte de detail est le religion de success."* (The pursuit of detail is the religion of success.)

At the time his ships were being built, Nazism was beginning to haunt the European continent and the imminence of war was causing the shipping industry to boom. Although they did not trade directly with the new German regime, many Greek shipowners, including Onassis, carried cargoes of ammunition and supplies for whomever could pay their tariff, and the Spanish Civil War, which started in 1936, also added to their increased business. Onassis made hundreds of thousands, if not millions, of dollars by having his freighters at the right place at the right time in the Mediterranean and the Atlantic.

In June 1938, as the effects of the Depression were beginning to wear off, the *Ariston* was completed. As part of the financing negotiation, it was registered in the country where it was built, and therefore flew the light blue and yellow crossed flag, with the royal crest of Sweden emblazoned on it.

The maiden voyage of the *Ariston* was a joyous one for Onassis. He invited his sisters Artemis and Merope and their husbands, Professor Theodore Garofalides and Nicholas Konialides, to cruise with him and Ingebord. Merope and Nicholas were newlyweds and the cruise was their honeymoon and the cause of much celebration. The ship left Goteborg, traveled across the Atlantic and through the Panama Canal. There was a portable pool set up on deck and everyone sunbathed and swam during the day. Onassis did strenuous calisthenics systematically, twice a day. At night, there was lavish dining, and Ingebord provided entertainment at the piano. Onassis himself played the piano on occasion. He had learned to play one piece with particular finesse, Bach's *Inventions*, which was his sole offering for the entire voyage. Twelve days after they had left Sweden, they arrived in San Francisco.

As soon as the *Ariston* docked in the United States, she began her first commercial service — nine consecutive voyages from San Francisco to Yokohama, one year's charter, issued by one of J. Paul Getty's subsidiaries, Tidewater Oil Company, to deliver oil to the Mitsuis Corporation of Japan. Onassis has often claimed that this first contract was probably the most important step he made in building his kingdom of tankers. His profit from that first year was $600,000. The *Ariston* had all but paid for itself.

Onassis escorted and invited his entourage from the *Ariston* on the first extensive trip through the United States that any of them had ever made. They traveled by train and to tourist attractions such as the city of New Orleans and the Grand Canyon, and spent several nights touring Chicago nightclubs. The trip ended in New York where they all stayed at the St. Moritz. Onassis later proclaimed it as one of his favorite New York hotels because its restaurant reminded him of a Parisian bistro. After spending their days touring Coney Island, the Statue of Liberty and Central Park, they dined at night at restaurants like the Colony and Chambord.

In 1939, at the time of Hitler's invasion of Poland, Onassis was in London, staying at the Savoy Hotel. Although it was practically impossible for aliens to leave or enter England, his Argentine diplomatic passport enabled him to secure permission to leave the country and travel by ship to Stockholm to discuss the future fate of his ships. The *Ariston* was flying Swedish colors and Sweden was neutral. The *Aristophanes* was a Greek ship and Greece was also neutral. Finally, the *Buenos Aires* had Argentine registry and Argentina was neutral, too. Onassis was optimistic about his shipping business, but soon

57

discovered that a Swedish-German agreement had been signed and all ships in Swedish ports had to remain where they were for the duration of the war. Unfortunately, his three ships were docked in Goteborg. With no alternative, Onassis was forced to depart from Sweden, leaving almost 50,000 tons of shipping potential idle until the conflict was ended. As Willi Frischauer, a long-time Onassis observer and chronicler of his exploits, states, "After fifteen years of almost unimpeded progress, these were the first real setbacks in the career of Aristotle Onassis. They were cruel blows." Indeed, although still the proprietor of enough ships to furnish himself with a generous income, he was nevertheless totally embittered after spending millions to build his fleet, only to see his prize ships and money-makers dormant. He left Sweden more determined than ever to succeed.

He returned to Buenos Aires and began to revitalize and restructure his tobacco business. Since no shipments from the East could be counted on because of the war, he made arrangements to have tobacco imported from Cuba and Brazil. All over the world, tobacco was beginning to become scarce, and people were willing to smoke almost any brand and even to roll their own, if necessary. Instead of suffering because he could no longer supply the market he had created for Oriental leaves, his business increased greatly because of the war rationing.

Even though his fleet had been markedly depleted, because of his inability to use his three supertankers, he put his remaining ships to profitable use sailing for the Allies and as a result collected unusually high wartime shipping rates. He made, as one critic described it, "oceans of money from the war," and under circumstances which some thought implied misconduct. Ernest Leiser, in an article in the *Saturday Evening Post*, was highly critical of the wartime shipping efforts of the Greek shipowners — including Onassis.

"Most of them offered their vessels as valuable — or so it seemed — additions to the Allied merchant fleets. To be sure, many of the ships were so decrepit that they were ideal torpedo bait.

An early photograph of Aristotle
Onassis as a young millionaire in
Buenos Aires, Argentina.
(Keystone)

Onassis' father, Socrates, was one
of the wealthiest businessmen in
the city of Smyrna in eastern
Turkey. Aristotle was also
born there.

Penelope Onassis died of uremic
poisoning at the age of 25 and her
husband, Socrates Onassis, later
remarried.

JUL 16 1942

PERSONAL AND CONFIDENTIAL
BY SPECIAL MESSENGER

Rear Admiral Emory S. Land
Administrator
War Shipping Administration
Department of Commerce Building
Washington, D. C.

My dear Admiral:

Information has been received from a confidential source
that Mr. Aristotelis Onassis, who is reportedly part owner of the
tankers "Calliroy" and "Antiope", was scheduled to depart for the
United States on Thursday, June 18, 1942, by Pan American clipper
from Buenos Aires, Argentina. According to the informant, the
purpose of Onassis' visit is to continue the negotiations for the
sale of these two tankers to the War Shipping Administration.

The informant advised there is no information available
indicating Mr. Onassis has any other motive for making a trip to the
United States, but it was reported he has expressed sentiments
inimical to the United States war effort, and that his activities
and movements while in the United States should be carefully
scrutinized.

Sincerely yours,

J. E. Hoover

John Edgar Hoover
Director

At the launching of one of his
super-tankers in Hamburg,
Germany, in 1954, Onassis poses
with his first wife, Tina Livanos
Onassis (who is using canes
because of a skiing accident), and
their two children, Alexander and
Christina.

(United Press International)

Before his relationship with Maria Callas, there were many happy years for Onassis and his beautiful young bride, Tina. Here they are in Paris in 1959.
(Jean-Pierre Rey—Gamma)

e world's most fabulous yacht, *Christina*, which at the cost of millions, Onassis verted into a floating palace. It was employed by Onassis as an important base hipping operations. He kept in touch with his offices all over the world through ship's ultrasophisticated communications system, but also used the *Christina* grand salon, where he would entertain the international jet set. *(Wide World Photos)*

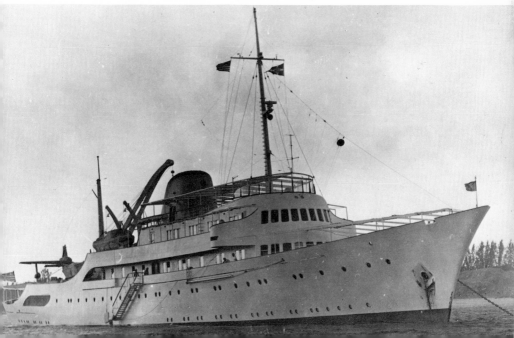

Virtually on a whim, in the early 1950s Onassis bought the bank at Monte Carlo and for several years dominated the social and financial scenes of the tiny kingdom of Monaco. Here, he and *La Callas* are flanked by Princess Grace and Prince Rainier, their constant companions. Eventually, a power struggle between the two men caused a break in the relationship.
(Gamma)

One of Onassis' closest friends was Winston Churchill, who spent virtually all of his holidays in his later years aboard Onassis' opulent yacht *Christina*. Here they are seen in 1960 after lunching at the Hotel de Paris in Monaco.
(Wide World Photos)

Here in 1957, Onassis drives Churchill on a sightseeing tour while on the island of Rhodes. Lady Churchill and Tina Onassis share the back seat.

(C. Megaloconomou/Authenticated News International)

Onassis and Maria Callas only have sunglassed eyes for each other as they engage in an intense toast with ouzo at an Athens restaurant in the early 1960s.
(Sipa-Press)

Onassis' relationship with the tempestuous opera diva Maria Callas kept gossip columnists in business for over a decade. This photo was taken in 1967 when the colorful couple docked in Nassau Harbor in the Bahamas. *(Wide World Photos)*

Although his marriage proposal to Elizabeth Taylor was rejected, Onassis continued to see and escort her whenever possible. Here the two share an evening at the annual ball of the Palace Rezzonico in Venice, 1967. *(Keystone)*

Onassis, with his sister Merope at his left, entertains Elizabeth Taylor and Richard Burton aboard the *Christina* during a visit to Monte Carlo. *(Sipa-Press)*

But, until they sank, they carried priceless cargoes across the sub-infested Atlantic. If they were useful to the Allied war efforts, they were even more useful to the ambitions of their owners. War zone rates were high. Besides, when one of these antiques sank, the insurance money sometimes would pay for a new one. It was, so to speak, expansion capital."

Despite the fact that he was realizing handsome profits from tobacco, in the middle of the war, 1942, Onassis suddenly moved his entire operation to New York, closing down his tobacco operation and concentrating almost all of his efforts on increasing his shipping interests in the area that he felt would net him much more profit. The move also enabled him to more closely supervise the operations of some of his tankers which were transporting oil from the tacky town of San Pedro, the port of Los Angeles, to Canada.

During his many trips to the West Coast, he always stayed at the swank and celebrity-conscious Beverly Hills Hotel in Los Angeles and quickly became involved with the Hollywood film colony, first through his fellow countryman and fellow shipowner, Spyros Skouras, the president of Twentieth Century-Fox. Through Skouras, he became friends with Alexis Minotis and his wife, Katina Paxinou, one of the finest actresses ever to appear on the modern Greek stage. She captured the attention of American movie fans in her role as Pilar in *For Whom the Bell Tolls*. He also spent much time with people like Otto Preminger, Ludwig Bemelmans and Simone Simone. A legend was beginning to grow: Onassis, the mysterious Greek shipping tycoon, rich as Croesus, with all the paraphernalia of success, would arrive in an outrageously luxurious chauffeur-driven limousine at the most lavish Hollywood parties and invariably give the hostess a token of his affection, a diamond bracelet worth thousands. The host would not be forgotten either, a silver, monogrammed cigarette case would be his, filled with Onassis' own privately selected and, during the war, impossible-to-get, Turkish cigarettes.

Often, Costa Gratsos, Onassis' old friend from

Buenos Aires, would travel down the coast from San Francisco, where he served as Greek Maritime Consul, to Los Angeles, where the two would participate in a constant round of parties and generally revel in the Hollywood high life. For the most part, though, they spent their time together talking of ships and shipping, as they always had, and comparing notes about the industry. Gratsos, like Onassis, had always wanted to go into the whaling business and soon he persuaded Onassis to participate in a small whaling operation. Both men would serve as equal partners. They had discovered an old whaling station in northern California, located less than 100 miles from the Oregon border, in a small town called Eureka. With the relatively insignificant sum of approximately $15,000, they chartered an old boat, hardly more than a scow, hired a Swedish gunner on a per diem basis and put on a minuscule crew. The boat would cruise up and down the West Coast searching for whales. Some thirty five were eventually killed. The whale meat was sold to nearby mink farms for feed and the whale livers were purchased by the Borden Co., which used them for a Vitamin A extract that they were manufacturing. The venture proved to be profitable, although not enormously so, and once again Onassis was convinced that whaling could eventually be a lucrative undertaking for him, despite the legend that only Scandinavians could operate a whaling fleet and hunt whales successfully.

Although his frequent trips to California usually proved to be both socially and financially rewarding, it was in New York, the largest American seaport and the cultural and society capital of the United States, that he flourished during the war in his personal and business life. He took a lavish suite on the thirty-seventh floor, high atop the Ritz Towers on Manhattan's 57th Street and Park Avenue. Among other celebrities, Greta Garbo was his neighbor. He wined and dined at El Morocco, the Stork Club, "21" and the Plaza. He and Ingebord stayed at the Ritz throughout the winters until April or May and spent the summers at a home he bought near Oyster Bay on Long Island which he christened "Mamita Cottage." He returned to Manhattan in the fall or only when business demanded it. Spyros Skouras had a large estate nearby, as did Alberto Dodero, Stavros Livanos, Stavros Niarchos and a number of other Greek and non-Greek ship-owners, and they formed an informal but closely knit social set and makeshift maritime business fraternity.

The wartime years that Onassis spent on Long Island were among the most happy of his life. It was the first permanent dwelling he had ever owned and the first time he had lived in a house, not an apartment, since he was a child in Smyrna. He waterskied, played tennis and Ping-Pong, entertained constantly, and was particularly proud of his French chef from Britanny who prepared superb gourmet meals.

He spent time taking long walks with his two dogs — humorously, one a cocker spaniel and the other a Great Dane — or speeding his Chris-Craft all over Long Island Sound. In the evenings, he usually played poker with Niarchos, Livanos and others. His relationship with Ingebord appeared sound for the moment and he did not attempt to hide the fact to anyone that he loved her. He gave her a rare yellow 13-carat diamond ring, worth tens of thousands of dollars, which he brought in from Argentina. He presented it to her wrapped in a handkerchief. "This is for you, Mamita. I want you to wear it always," he said. Decades later, it was still on her finger. She has claimed that he proposed marriage a number of times, offering her a million dollars as a dowry if she consented.

Ingebord remained loyal to Onassis even though there were times when she felt she should have left him. She relates a story that one evening they dined with Stavros Niarchos at Lloyds Neck and she was dressed in bright green-striped pants. Onassis was visibly annoyed with her clothing, but said nothing until they returned home.

He was furious about the way she looked, "Why do you dress in this abominable fashion?" he screamed. "Where did you find these abominable pants? Did you think we were going to a circus? You really want me to look ridiculous!" He then battered her across the room with his fists, kicking her when she fell to the floor.

The next day Onassis was uncontrite. "All Greek husbands, I tell you, all Greek men, without exception, beat their wives. It's good for them." Ingebord accepted the

61

"apology." She also said that his occasional bouts of jealousy would send him into a rage. After she was driven home by a Yugoslavian shipowner from a party which Onassis could not attend, Onassis pummeled her so badly that the next day he embarrassedly dismissed the servants for the remainder of the week, so that they could not see her bruises. After that incident, some of her friends and her doctor urged and insisted that she leave him, but she still remained with him.

For the first time in his adult life, he worked very little and still managed to accumulate large profits. Several of his ships had been chartered to the U.S. Maritime Commission and each were making him close to $250,000 a year. His total obligation was to collect the green-colored checks sent to him each month by the U.S. government. Of his other ships, those with Panamanian registry had continued to operate throughout the war at great profits.

With the increased success he was experiencing because of the war, however, came suspicion in some quarters. Over 450 Greek ships participated in the war on the side of the Allies and fully 360 of them were sunk with thousands of Greek merchant seamen losing their lives. Onassis, of all the major Greek shipowners in the war, had not lost a single sailor, nor one ship; and the profits he was making began to look mysteriously fortuitous. It was known that he was close to the Argentine government and some people believed he was pro-Nazi. Alberto Dodero, who was his neighbor and very close friend, was on intimate terms with Eva Peron, and although neutral, Argentina leaned more heavily toward the Axis during World War II and eventually became a haven for Nazis during and after the war. There was even a heavily circulated rumor that Onassis was conducting a clandestine affair with Madame Peron. Although there was no direct proof of any misdeeds on his part, a secret investigation was begun, and for the duration of the war Onassis, without his knowledge, was put under constant surveillance by the F.B.I. As a result of that agency's interest in Onassis, the Foreign Funds Control Division of the Treasury Department also began its own observation of him and his financial transactions for the remainder of the war. The investigations became even more active when it was learned that he had a brief affair with Maria Constantinesco, a known spy for the Germans who was later convicted and imprisoned. His case was considered important enough to come under the direct supervision of J. Edgar Hoover, who wrote the following letter:

Federal Bureau of Investigation
United States Department'of Justice
Washington, D.C.
July 16, 1942
PERSONAL AND CONFIDENTIAL
BY SPECIAL MESSENGER

Rear Admiral Emory S. Land
Administrator
War Shipping Administration
Department of Commerce Building
Washington, D.C.

My dear Admiral:

Information has been received from a confidential source that Mr. Aristotelis Onassis, who is reportedly part owner of the tankers "Calliroy" and "Antiope", was scheduled to depart for the United States on Thursday, June 18, 1942, by Pan American clipper from Buenos Aires, Argentina. According to the informant, the purpose of Onassis' visit is to continue the negotiations for the sale of these two tankers to the War Shipping Administration.

The informant advised there is no information available indicating Mr. Onassis has any other motive for making a trip to the United States, but it was reported he has expressed sentiments inimical to the United States war effort, and that his activities and movements while in the United States should be carefully scrutinized.

Sincerely yours,

John Edgar Hoover
Director

Although the surveillance cost the American taxpayers tens of thousands of dollars as Onassis traveled from New York to Beverly Hills and back again, nothing was ever discovered

63

about his activities that enabled the F.B.I. or any other governmental department to bring any action against him for
treasonous wartime machinations. By the time the war was
over, his fortune was estimated at $30 million.

6

One afternoon during the first weeks of 1947, Eva Peron
flashed her dark eyes at Aristotle Onassis and scrutinized his
child-wife, Tina, who was then seventeen years old, as the
couple climbed the gangplank of Alberto Dodero's legendary sailing yacht.

Evita, as she was called, was a former actress who
had organized mass demonstrations on behalf of her
husband, Juan Peron, to have him released from prison,
and later helped him to become elected President of Argentina. However, it was she who practically governed the
country. She was a brilliant strategist, a fiery orator, and a
woman of great political passion and ambition.

Dodero, who had accompanied her on her spec-
tacular tour of Europe, had asked her, as a favor, to take a
short cruise to help him persuade Onassis to buy the

financially draining Argentine Navigation Line, which Dodero then owned.

Evita wanted Onassis' money in Argentina, and she began talking business almost as soon as he came aboard. Attractive, at twenty-six she was one of the most famous and powerful women in the world. Onassis listened, and studied her.

Also aboard was the colorful Fritz Mandl, former president of one of the largest fabric corporations in Germany and an owner of an airplane plant in Argentina. He was the husband of Hedy Lamarr.

Dodero and Evita attempted to persuade, cajole, bully and charm both men to go into partnership and buy the navigation company. The alcohol flowed, the setting was idyllic, Onassis felt almost weak from the force of Evita. He wanted to sleep with her, despite the fact that his marriage was not yet one-month old. Tina stayed dutifully in the background as the talks progressed.

Onassis sensed something suspicious about Evita's insistence. She was asking for millions of dollars—almost more than he could afford—and there were no guarantees of any kind given or even implied. Yet he had no information to indicate that the deal she and Dodero offered was not as potentially lucrative as they promised. Finally, acting purely on instinct, he refused to participate.

Evita was furious, but remained outwardly polite. Only her eyes showed the anger she felt. She smiled at him, and then turned her full attention to Mandl. Mandl invested almost all of his vast holdings.

Within one year, the Peron government national-ized several major companies, including the Argentine Navigation Line, and Mandl's investment was completely wiped out.

The first Onassis-owned ship to leave Piraeus at the immediate conclusion of the war and sail the U-boat-free Atlantic con-tained over a dozen of his relatives, including two of his sisters and a bevy of nieces, nephews, aunts and uncles. In New York, they were reunited with Onassis and told tales of the starvation, the violence, and the resistance movement of the three-year reign of Nazi- and Italian-occupied Greece. Onassis also had the *Ariston* released from its dockings in Norway and brought to New York, and when it arrived, a shipboard party to celebrate the family's reunion went on for days.

One of the first things that Onassis discussed with his sister Artemis, his lifelong confidante, was his emotional life.

According to Greek familial tradition, a son is not to marry until all of the daughters have been betrothed, and in Onassis' case, since all three sisters had taken husbands, he was now free to take a wife. He was nearing forty and he thought the time was close for marriage. His fortune was continuing to increase and he wanted a son, an heir, to carry on his name and business. For whatever reason, Ingebord would not consent to cement their relationship, much as he had wanted it, and now he had begun to think that the five-year difference in their ages—she was older—would adversely affect their getting on permanently. But aside from that, he felt somewhat culturally dominated by Ingebord and wanted to begin to stand on his own. Although Artemis had always been fond of Ingebord, she could understand her brother's concern. When he talked of other possible marriage partners with her, almost as if he were talking over the purchase of a ship, she gave him her advice. Marry a Greek girl, someone who can empathize with you and talk your language, figuratively and literally, and you will be much happier. Onassis needed no convincing because he had already begun spending time with Tina, age seventeen, and Eugenie, nineteen, the two daughters of Stavros G. Livanos, owner of the largest private fleet in the world and a consummate Greek. At that time, Livanos was so wealthy that he could have easily acquired all of Onassis' holdings for cash, without markedly tampering with his own assets.

Onassis had met Livanos and his wife when, after a short stay in Montreal, they moved to New York from London in 1942. Not only did Livanos control a vast shipping empire, but he had spent years on the sea himself, first as a deckhand when he was a boy, and finally as a captain of one of his father's ships. He held a master mariner's certificate and nothing pleased him more than to talk for hours about ships and the sea. He liked Onassis, except for one strong reservation.

Livanos was almost paranoiacally opposed to any kind of personal publicity, and although he was beseiged by reporters from all over the world eager to do a profile of him, he never consented to an interview. Onassis, conversely, was interested in personal publicity. His name had begun to appear in gossip columns, but he was still unknown by the general public, and he welcomed most opportunities to gain stories about himself in the press.

Livanos went to great lengths to avoid publicity. He maintained a huge, impenetrable suite at the top of the Plaza Hotel in New York, at a reported cost of $1,000 a day. Only his Greek friends were ever invited there. For additional seclusion, he had a vacation house near Oyster Bay on Long Island. Onassis was his neighbor there.

Onassis had first met the Livanos sisters on Saturday, April 17, 1943, a date that was vivid to him for many years to come. Livanos had invited Onassis, Niarchos, and a number of other Greek ship-owners to dine with him at the Plaza. Before dinner, Livanos served drinks in his library and the two girls — Tina, then fourteen, and Eugenie, sixteen — were proudly brought in and introduced to the small party. Onassis was immediately impressed and attracted to the girls who were beautiful, poised, and sophisticated young ladies. Tina had been born in Kensington, England, and baptized "Athena." Her governess always called her "Atina" and that was finally shortened to "Tina." Her great dream was to work in a laboratory, and she was studying chemistry, physics and biology in order to do so. Both sisters spoke with attractive British accents, had been educated at the finest English schools and at Miss Hewitt's Classes in New York. Years later, Tina remarked, "When I first saw Mr. Onassis, I remember being very impressed and somewhat intimidated."

During that summer and the two years following, Onassis, intrigued with and attracted to both girls, spent time waterskiing, swimming, and motor boating with them. The twenty-odd year difference in their ages didn't seem to matter. Since Onassis played poker at least once a week with Livanos, he would always see the two girls on that evening as a matter of course, and would meet them occasionally during the day as the summers progressed. Although no formal "dating" ever took place, and all meetings were chaperoned, it soon became apparent to everyone that he was very interested in both girls. The question was, which one? Ingebord, incensed by the competition, and sensing the end of the relationship with Onassis, moved out of "Mamita Cottage" and on her own rented a duplex in Manhattan. Onassis continued to see her but only sporadically, and then callously would often discuss his other relationships with her, including how he felt about Tina and Eugenie.

It was about that time that Onassis began to wear dark glasses, extra wide at the sides, which gave him a sinister look. It was believed that he had developed an eye ailment of sensitivity to the light, but some of his critics thought it was an affectation, adopted from his friends in Hollywood, used merely to impress, to indicate to the world that he was "somebody." It was for none of these reasons. Onassis once explained that his eyes were too expressive — he was continually revealing himself — and since he was often engaged in conversations where intent and nuance affected meaning to the tune of millions, he preferred to keep his true feelings, as phrased by his eyes, secret. Deep down, beneath the glasses, there was a great fever of thought and a constant, frenetic observation of everything around him. He was to continue this "disguise" for the rest of his life, only removing his dark glasses when he worked alone or when he had his photo taken, but insisting on wearing them in darkened nightclubs and even when he swam!

Another idiosyncrasy that he adopted around then was his failure ever to wear a topcoat even in the coldest weather. He once explained why: "Since I have a chauffeur-driven limousine, I rarely have to be out in the cold for more than a few seconds. I also go to ten or more nightclubs or restaurants in the course of an average day. Since I am known as a "rich" person, I feel I have to tip at least $5.00 each time I check my coat. On top of that, I would have to wear a very expensive coat, and it would have to be insured. Added up, without a top coat, I save over $20,000 a year!"

Livanos was eager to have Onassis as a son-in-law and began suggesting—without direct reference to his own daughters—that he consider getting married.

Eventually, in the fall of 1945, Onassis wrote a letter to Livanos asking him for his consent to marry Tina. Livanos was outraged that Onassis had not chosen Eugenie, his oldest daughter. There is an old Greek superstition that daughters must marry in order of seniority, so that a younger sister is not entitled to agree to an engagement while an elder sister remains single. If the younger sister marries first, it is believed that the elder will be doomed to spinsterhood. Livanos argued that Onassis was old enough to be Tina's father—he was 39, she was 16—although Livanos was more than twenty years older than his own wife. In reality, as Onassis put it, "Livanos thought it fitting and proper," again with a maritime analogy, "that the first off the line should be the first disposed of." Livanos was angered and did not deign to answer Onassis' letter, and he at first forbade Tina to see or speak to him. It took almost a year before Livanos accepted the inevitable: Tina and Ari were truly in love; Eugenie, although she was fond of Onassis, was "secretly" seeing Niarchos and the possibility of their marriage was very strong. Although Niarchos was married, it appeared that he might divorce his wife, Melponee, and marry Eugenie. Livanos gave in to Onassis when he learned of Niarchos' interest in Eugenie, and withdrew his objections to Tina marrying the man she wanted.

The formal engagement was announced in October 1946, and on December 28 of that year, Tina, wearing a resplendent wedding gown, and Onassis, dressed in a morning coat and sporting a white carnation, were married in a Greek Orthodox ceremony in New York. One of the officiating priests was Father Euthimion, a refugee from Smyrna and Onassis' former theology teacher at St. Paraskevis'.

The reception, an elegant affair, was held in the Grand Ballroom of the Plaza Hotel and Livanos' gift to the couple was a former World War II Liberty ship, after taxes and finance payments were made, worth over $100,000. Their

70

honeymoon was spent in Palm Beach and Key West, Florida, and in Buenos Aires, where Spyros Skouras and his wife were vacationing; they accompanied the newlyweds everywhere.

Alberto Dodero, who was one of the Long Island set of expatriate shipowners, invited Tina and Ari to be his guests at his palatial retreat, Bet Alba, in Montevideo and on his yacht which cruised up and down Rio de la Plata. Eva Peron, a close friend of Dodero's wife, Betty, was often aboard for the festivities. The time spent cruising on the yacht was not all pleasure, however. Dodero, together with Madame Peron, attempted to persuade Onassis to buy his ailing shipping company, and the two men talked night after night, usually until dawn, about the possibility. In the end Onassis refused the offer, appraising it as too much of a risk, even for him.

Back in New York, Tina and Ari moved into a lavish four-story townhouse at one of the city's most prestigious addresses, 16 Sutton Square, another surprise gift to the couple from Livanos—the price, $460,000. Onassis spent millions in redecorating and furnishing it.

Six months after Tina and Ari married, Niarchos and Eugenie were also wedded.

With the marriages by Onassis and Niarchos to the two Livanos sisters, there began a rivalry between the two brothers-in-law that would last a lifetime. The catalyst behind their contretemps was Onassis' belief that Tina was attracted to suave, handsome, man-of-the-world Niarchos. Onassis was almost insanely jealous, even when Tina just talked with Niarchos. Hoping for a complete schism between Niarchos and himself, and consequently Tina and Niarchos, Onassis forbade Tina to attend her sister's wedding. She did not go. This public humiliation, the first of many that would be exchanged by both men, incited hatred. They did have a rivalry for money that transcended their personal bitterness. Perhaps both had once read and been affected by H. L. Mencken's definition of wealth, "Any income that is at least $100 more a year than the income of one's wife's sister's husband."

Onassis and Niarchos first met in Greece in 1934. Stavros Spiros Niarchos was two years younger than Onassis.

When they met, Onassis was already a millionaire and known in Athens as a "personality." Niarchos was still a struggling young businessman. Both men had, even at the time, what the other wanted. Onassis had success in business but was still rough-hewn. He had not yet met Ingebord Dedichen and was a bit frayed in social situations. Niarchos was deeply entrenched in Athens society, drove a Bugatti, owned a sleek yacht, paid for by his family, dressed like a men's fashion model, and had the *savoir faire* of an experienced man of the world.

As the years progressed, this theme of jealousy would express itself again and again as Onassis attempted to be "accepted" in society, like Niarchos, and Niarchos attempted to make "as much" money as Onassis. Despite the Greek tradition that *batzanskia* (men who marry sisters) should act like brothers, the two men continued feuding with only occasional respite. As Onassis once stated in an interview that appeared in the *London Times*, "In business we cut each other's throats, but now and then we sit around the same table and behave, for the sake of the ladies."

Each extra dollar Onassis made was considered grounds for a personal grudge by Niarchos and each time Niarchos' name appeared in a society column, Onassis felt diminished. But envy makes strange bedfellows, and as they continued to compete, their lives constantly interwove in a series of defeats and victories for first one, then the other.

The Livanos-Onassis-Niarchos family dynasty was the most formidable shipowning clan the world had ever seen with over a billion dollars of combined assets, and the "mergers" caused great stirrings throughout the shipping industry. It was believed that the marriages, like Onassis' ships of convenience, were arranged for financial purposes. Although Livanos was generous to both of his sons-in-law with substantial wedding gifts, he considered them business rivals and competitors and at no time were any financial favors requested, given, or even mentioned.

At first, Niarchos and Onassis pooled a few of their dry cargo ships in a new company that they organized to take advantage of the post-war shipping boom, but within a very short while neither could agree on the scope, method or direction of their joint venture and the cooperative liaison was abandoned.

Onassis desperately wanted more ships and more tonnage to add to his fleet. Although American shipyards were eager to initiate special deals at bargain prices to build new ships, his interest lay elsewhere—U.S. government-owned Liberty ships. Some 5,425 cargo ships had been constructed during the war years and of those that were not sunk by the enemy or battered apart by heavy seas due to hasty and faulty welding, thousands still remained. With the war over, the government had no further use for them. The Federal Maritime Commission made an attempt to sell the ships to American shipping operators at discount prices, but the operators failed to see the potential in the purchase and reconditioning of these ships. It appeared that the ships would be left to rust under Government expense—and acres of them began to accumulate on the rivers and in the harbors all over the country.

Onassis was eager to buy as many Liberty ships as he could for conversion to his fleet. Employing a business principle that he would use over and over again throughout his career, he attempted to buy the ships without using his own capital or assets but by simply borrowing the funds that he needed.

Using his townhouse on Sutton Square as a business salon, Onassis entertained the business community of New York City, looking for the money that he needed. The parties were lavish. Actors and actresses, athletes and writers, mingled with bankers, financial executives, shipping tycoons. "It got so that almost every time you turned around one of Onassis' men was inviting you to another party at Sutton Square," said one oil company executive. "And I must admit, I never missed one."

It was not a simple maneuver. Although he was rich, the banks and insurance companies considered the shipping business to be too erratic, too subject to strikes and the vagaries of war, weather and wages for them to become interested in investing in Onassis' company. Finally, after many rejections, he persuaded the president of the National City Bank to lend him half of the money needed to buy sixteen Liberty ships, mainly because he had already convinced the U.S. government officials that his shipping corporation was the most reliable and experienced to carry coal and other necessities to the devastated countries of Europe under the energetic and sympathetic post-war U.S. aid program. Thousands of ships would be needed and Onassis had every intention of being the owner of many of them. There was one problem with Onassis' plan. The Ship Sales Act of 1946 forbade the sale of tankers and other ships to foreigners. They could only be sold to American citizens or to corporations controlled by U.S. citizens. Onassis attempted to circumvent the Act, but until such time as he could determine a secure method of doing so, he set out to increase his oil tanker business.

He attempted to interest large oil companies in carrying their oil in his tankers at a set price that would not fluctuate during the term of the contract, a period of from three to five years. Most oil companies did not have enough tankers of their own to transport all the oil that was being ordered, so Onassis' guaranteed shipping prices, at lower "flag of convenience" prices than could be secured from American shippers, were highly attractive to them. Since shipping rates were always on the increase, the signing of such a long-term fixed contract appeared to be advantageous. If oil prices dropped, however, the oil companies would have to pay more under the contract than on the open market. It was a calculated gamble for them, but one worth taking.

To ensure that such long-term contracts would remain profitable for him regardless of possible fluctuations in shipping rates, Onassis wanted to build the largest and most modern tanker in the world, one so efficient and profitable that it would have virtually no competitors. To finance the building of the ship, he used a contract he had secured from the Mobil Oil Company which consisted of a five-year charter for a 28,000-ton tanker. The Metropolitan Life Insurance Company, assured by the Mobil contract, financed the building of such a ship at a cost of $2 million.

Soon Texaco followed suit with another long-term

contract, which further improved Onassis' borrowing power. More money was loaned by the Chase Manhattan and the Chemical banks of New York, and he eventually had five supertankers — the largest in the world — under construction at a cost of $40 million. Onassis had not advanced one cent of his own money to build any of them.

With his oil-tanker business burgeoning, he returned to the problem of securing the Liberty ships. Working with a small army of attorneys, the question Onassis asked was how could one determine the nationality of a corporation. Certainly an individual's citizenship was a matter of record, but it is more difficult to determine the citizenship of a multinational corporation. If 51 percent of the corporate stock is owned by Americans, then that corporation must certainly be American. The remaining 49 percent of the stock could be controlled by anyone, or so it appeared. Originally Onassis thought he would operate the ships under his usual method of flags of convenience. He had ships registered not only in Panama, but in Honduras and Liberia as well; but to secure the Liberty ships, he knew that they would have to be registered under a U.S. flag with an all-American crew. The profits that could be made were still so great that abandoning his usual method of registration didn't stop him from trying to secure the ships.

While American shipowners were reluctant to purchase the tankers and dry-cargo ships, both Niarchos and Onassis were burning to take advantage of the unprecedented sale. Niarchos acted first. He established, in New York, the North American Shipping and Trading Company (N.A.S.T.C.), in which he owned 40 percent of the stock, while the remaining 60 percent was controlled by four U.S. citizens, including Niarchos' sister, Mrs. Andrew Dracopoulos.

At the same time, Niarchos became associated with a powerful economic, military, and legal group of influential Americans, known as the Casey group. Members of that group included ex-Congressman Joseph E. Casey, a Massachusetts Democrat; a former Secretary of State, Edward R. Stettinius; Brig. General Julius Holmes; and Fleet Admiral William ("Bull") Halsey. In a byzantine fashion, the Casey group, in

1947, formed the American Overseas Tanker Corporation which bought five T-2 tankers from the U.S. government. The Overseas Tanker Corporation transferred its ships to the Greenwich Marine Company registered in Panama. Then a Niarchos-connected corporation, the Delaware Tanker Corporation, controlled by Americans, purchased the American Overseas Tanker Corporation. Niarchos' World Tanker Company then bought the stock of the Greenwich Marine and the five T-2 tankers were now under Niarchos' control. Other corporate transactions gave Niarchos an additional nine T-2 surplus tankers.

Onassis, following Niarchos' example, organized the United States Petroleum Carriers, Inc., which purchased, along with its subsidiary, Victory Carriers, Inc., 14 T-2 tankers, 7 victory ships and 2 Liberty ships. The Casey group also assisted Onassis in completing his transactions with the U.S. Government. Onassis' companies, like those of Niarchos, were registered in Panama.

Onassis, working within legal safeguards, owned a *safe* 49 percent of the stock of the United States Petroleum Carriers, Inc. The rest of the company stock was owned by American citizens.

Onassis and Niarchos were enjoying the profits of their newly reconditioned U.S. Government ships until a series of U.S. Government hearings, chaired by Senator Clyde Howey (D-North Carolina), attempted to prove that the Greek shipowners had deceived the U.S. Government.

Committee hearings in 1951 and 1952 demonstrated that the surplus ships, which had originally been purchased by American-controlled corporations, had slipped into alien hands; a later indictment charged that false financial statements had been filed, The members of the committee disclosed information about the Casey group which made a $3,250,000 profit on an investment of $101,000 in two surplus ship transactions. At the time of the hearings, the names of the Greek shipowners were rarely discussed.

A Federal grand jury was called to investigate the information compiled by the Howey Committee. Even infamous Senator Joseph McCarthy shouted his way into the act

76

with his subcommittee, charging that some of the Onassis-owned ships carried cargoes to Communist China and also between iron-curtain countries. Nothing came of the Senator's personal barrages, however.

It was not until April 23, 1953, that the grand jury drew up its indictments—32 persons including Onassis and Niarchos and 18 corporations were named. The indictments were not made public until almost a year later on February 23, 1954.

Niarchos heard about the indictments in 1953 through his international grapevine and did not leave his London home.

Onassis, on the other hand, wanted to confront the U.S. government head-on. "My 49 percent share does not constitute control," declared Onassis. Nevertheless, he was indicted by the District of Columbia grand jury on October 13, 1953. The following February 4, Onassis cabled the U.S. Attorney General: I WISH TO INFORM YOU THAT HAVING ARRIVED FROM EUROPE ON MONDAY NIGHT, I PLACE MYSELF AT YOUR DISPOSAL DURING MY VISIT IN THIS COUNTRY FOR ANY INFORMATION YOU OR YOUR DEPARTMENT MIGHT CARE TO HAVE.

When Onassis received no response to his telegram, he barged into Attorney General Leo Rover's office on February 8. "I want to know what this indictment is all about," he demanded. "Let's have a showdown here and now." The Attorney General excused himself, left the office and returned with a U.S. marshal who placed Onassis into custody. He, thus, became one of the richest men in U.S. history ever to be arrested. After being numbered, photographed and finger-printed, Onassis pleaded innocent and was released on a $10,000 bond. Onassis was forbidden to leave the country until his trial but somehow managed to have that order changed. He began traveling as usual, but promised to be back one month ahead of his trial date.

Onassis and eight codefendants were charged with conspiracy to violate the false statement statute of the Ship Sales Act. They were also indicted for falsifying balance sheets and financial statements and making incorrect statements about citizenship. The maximum penalty for each count of the indictment was five years' imprisonment, a $10,000 fine or both. Onassis' chief codefendants were ex-Congressman Casey and Robert L. Berenson, chairman of the board of the United States Petroleum Carriers. (On January 4, 1954, the Washington grand jury also indicted five other Greek shipping operators including Manuel E. Kulukundis, chairman of the New York Greek Shipowners Committee.)

On February 8, Onassis released the following statement to the press:

"While I was in Europe, reports reached me that several sealed indictments had been obtained by the Department of Justice in which I might have been included. As soon as possible, and without being summoned or even requested to appear, I returned voluntarily to the United States to find out whether I was involved and if so to clear my name.

"The indictment has now been unsealed. It appears that the Government now claims that transactions, which it previously sanctioned as lawful and even encouraged, might be unlawful.

"The simple facts are these. United States Petroleum Carriers, Inc., an American corporation, was organized in 1947 by a group of American citizens to purchase and operate vessels. Sometime later, a foreign corporation, which I represent, was offered by the American group and acquired a 49 percent stock interest in the American company, as permitted by the shipping laws. The Maritime Commission was immediately advised of the participation of the foreign group. With the shipping know-how, funds and collateral provided by the foreign company I represent, purchase of vessels was made possible. United States Petroleum Carriers bought more than twenty vessels representing a total tonnage of over 300,000 deadweight tons, over a period of three years. All vessel purchases were fully reviewed by the Legal Division of the U.S. Maritime Commission, after close scrutiny and investigation of the Company, its officers and its citizen and foreign stockholders. These purchases were further approved by the Board of Maritime Commissioners as well as by leading private counsel for the Company and the lending institutions. All subsequent operations of the vessels have been conducted under Maritime Commission regulations which require monthly disclosure of conditions to the Commission.

"The resulting enterprise represented a total investment in vessels of about $30,000,000 most of which has been paid in cash. From these vessels, the Company and its subsidiaries derived gross revenues of over $50,000,000 and an operating profit of over $20,000,000. About $30,000,000 was paid in wages to American crews and to American businessmen for supplies, equipment and repairs. Millions of dollars were paid in American taxes. Except for modest regular dividends paid to stockholders, the profits of United States Petroleum Carriers were left with it to help finance expansion.

"This successful shipping operation was at all times beneficially owned and controlled by American citizens owning 51 percent of the stock. At all times, 100 percent of the stock of United States Petroleum Carriers has been in the custody of an American bank under an agreement between the stockholders assuring continued American control of the Company. The ships carried millions of tons of defense cargoes, and gave employment to more than a thousand American seamen. Through the sale of surplus vessels to the Company, the Government recovered for U.S. taxpayers two thirds of the original cost of constructing the vessels, as against the usual realization of less than one tenth of cost in dispositions of used surplus property. Instead of rusting in muddy rivers at the expense of the taxpayers, as thousands of unsold Government vessels still are, the ships purchased by United States Petroleum Carriers carried the flag of the American merchant marine throughout the world, fully equipped, manned entirely by American crews, and instantaneously available to the U.S. Government in the event of national emergency.

"The Government now takes the position that this enterprise which it had repeatedly sanctioned, and which served the country so well, might be unlawful. Having treated the Company as a citizen-buyer with full knowledge of the foreign interest, the Government now asserts that the Company did not qualify as a citizen, and that vessels which the Government itself sold time after time to the Company are forfeitable to the Government without return of the purchase price. Without establishing the justice of its position which is still to be tested in the courts, the Government has seized the vessels and impounded their revenues. Further, the Government now claims that the open association between the American and foreign groups was an unlawful conspiracy, although the facts were fully known to and accepted repeatedly by the Maritime Commission which continued to sell ships to the Company year after year in accordance with its then existing policy. In fact, the Commission sold vessels to United States Petroleum Carriers as late as 1951.

"My good name in the United States means a great deal to me. My wife and two children are American citizens. My relationships with American businessmen and with the Government have been a source of pride to me. Shortly after World War II, it was my good fortune to be able to prevent the shutting down of one of the finest American shipyards—the Bethlehem Yards at Sparrows Point—by placing with them an order for construction of the first fleet of supertankers. At the outbreak of the Korean War, I offered unconditionally my entire foreign fleet, together with my whaling fleet, and also my personal services and resources, to the United States Navy for the duration of the emergency—an offer which I believe was made by no other shipowner, and for which I was officially thanked by the Navy. Years before, the Senate investigated shipments to Communist China, and before there was any governmental opposition to such trade, it was my firm policy to refuse all cargoes destined for Iron Curtain countries, including North Korea and Communist China.

"Despite the apparent unfairness of bringing charges against any man for transactions such as these conducted openly and in good faith, I have returned, without compulsion, to put an end to unfounded and vicious rumors. I shall be glad to have the issues determined by the courts in accordance with the fine traditions of American Justice."

After the Onassis indictment was made public, he made no attempt to conceal the fact that he was, indeed, the chief power behind the United States Petroleum Carriers, even though he owned a mere 49 percent of that company's stock. He told the press that "because the American citizens who were the controlling stockholders in Petroleum Carriers didn't have the money while I had it, they came to me and I lent it to them." Onassis' co-defendant, ex-Congressman Casey, was dismissed of all charges in the Washington Federal Court, because he was granted immunity for testimony he provided a Federal grand jury about the quasi-legal shipping transactions.

As the U.S. courts were fighting the Greek ship-owners, the Justice Department began seizing the surplus ships as they entered U.S. ports. By the end of February 1954, the U.S. Government had successfully recovered 47 tankers and dry cargo ships which were then under alien control.

Niarchos was also one of the major employers of shipbuilders in the United States. In 1952, he signed a $10 million contract with Bethlehem Steel Company for a major tanker to be constructed in Quincy, Mass. — enough work to employ over 1,000 men for several years. In 1953, he placed a tentative order with Bethlehem for two additional ships. When Niarchos learned of his indictments, he announced that he would halt any shipbuilding contracts currently held with Bethlehem.

The American shipbuilding industry was faced with a severe post-war depression and Niarchos' decision would permanently cripple the industry and unemployment rates would reach new heights. In light of Niarchos' decision, the United States Government decided to negotiate with the Greek shipping magnate.

L. E. P. Taylor, Niarchos' British attorney, and Warren Burger, U.S. Assistant Attorney General, began months of negotiations. They concluded that:

Niarchos would return 19 of the surplus vessels to the U.S. Government; Niarchos would pay the U.S. government $110,000 in fines levied against 7 of his companies; Niarchos would pay the U.S. government $4 million, a share of the profits made while the U.S. ships flew under Niarchos' flags; all charges against individuals would be dropped; ships would not be surrendered for a period of 90 days.

This would give the Maritime Administration time to make a possible exchange deal. New contracts for the construction of American tonnage would be exchanged for a transference of 19 ships to a "friendly foreign flag." If the ships were to be surrendered to the United States, all mortgage payments still due ($7,700,000) were to be canceled. The U.S. government promised to transfer the ships to a "friendly foreign flag," if Niarchos would help bail out the sagging economy of the American shipbuilding industry.

In spite of the millions of dollars in fines and the loss of his ships, Niarchos did not fare badly in the government settlement. Profits in the industry were extremely high after World War II and the surplus ships paid for themselves more than a few times. Onassis was outraged that Niarchos gave in to the Americans. After the Niarchos settlement, the U.S. government began dismissing charges against the other individuals indicted.

On January 7, 1955, Kulukundis' charges were dropped, because he had previously testified before a grand jury about the Shipping Act transactions and was granted immunity. The Justice Department, however, continued to seize the U.S. surplus ships controlled by alien nations. Eventually, they seized 43 ships.

Ari's troubles were not over. In November 1954, the Justice Department filed a recovery suit for the $20 million profit which the Onassis' surplus war vessels had acquired during the post-war years. The suit was not filed against Onassis, but against his brother-in-law, Nicholas Konialides of Uruguay, and his wife, Merope. They were the financial custodians of the Onassis empire.

One of the more bizarre aspects of Onassis' difficulties with the Justice Department was his relationship with Herbert Brownell, a New York attorney, who was then Attorney General. Brownell's law firm, Lord, Day and Lord, experts in maritime law, had served as Onassis' attorneys advising him to buy the surplus tankers. As Attorney General, Brownell handed down the indictments against Onassis and later testified as a witness on behalf of Onassis, marking the first time in U.S. jurisprudence when an Attorney General was a defense witness in a case he himself was prosecuting.

In December 1955, the suit was settled. Onassis agreed to contract the construction of $50 million worth of ships in the U.S. He also consented to a complete overhaul of his American companies which were to be placed under U.S. control. Onassis was allowed to keep his surplus ships and put them under foreign registry. Even if he had forfeited them, he would have realized at least a $1 million profit on each of the ships.

7

Onassis sat cross-legged on a huge, tapestried cushion in the incensed, marble stateroom of King Saud of Saudi Arabia. After a long talk in Arabic, the two men sat in silence. Then, his eyes flashing, the King nodded, raised his hands to chest height and brought his two index fingers together side-by-side, indicating union and understanding. A short, brass table was placed before Onassis, and an aide quickly brought in a golden pen and the newly-worded contract:

"I, Aristotle S. Onassis, shall have the right to combine the company whose head office will be in Saudi Arabia with one or more of the companies a majority of whose shares are directly or indirectly owned by myself or by members of my family of Greek origin, provided that Jews have no direct or indirect interest in any of these companies. I further agree that the company shall not deal with Israel."

Onassis studied the document for just a second, smiled at the King, and signed it, without hesitation.

The summer of 1950 saw the beginning of the Korean War and once again, the shipping industry became a crucial factor in the success, or failure of the outcome of the conflict. The post-war controls over the great shipyards at Hamburg, Bremen and Kiel were immediately lifted and Onassis took instant advantage in placing orders at low prices with speedy delivery dates.

Before he was finished, Onassis had ordered over $75 million worth of ships to be built in Germany and almost single-handedly bolstered the ravaged post-war German shipping trade. His order for ships was the single largest non-military contract in German history and as a result, he became something of a national hero to them and certainly a celebrity. He also continued to endear himself to the Germans by flying an entire crew from Germany to Baltimore to take over the first voyage of his 28,000-ton tanker *Olympic Flame*, built at the Bethlehem Steel Yards. It incensed American seamen. A protest was staged, the American seamen threatened violence to the Germans and to "take over" the ship by force. Although the incident made headlines in the United States, eventually it calmed down and the *Olympic Flame* was launched with the Germans aboard. Onassis said he hired them because they all had "high pressure experience — what is needed at this time."

Traveling back and forth to Germany from his offices in New York, London and Paris, Onassis was often a personal guest of Konrad Adenaur and then Ludwig Erhard when he became chancellor of West Germany, both men eager to keep Onassis' millions pouring into their country.

Onassis' first two ships built in Germany, more than 45,000 tons each, were built in Hamburg. He also constructed a series of fast, less-than-gigantic sized (21,350 tons each) tankers, built by the A. G. Weser Shipyard of Bremen and by the Kiel Division of Howaldtswerke, one of the largest shipyards in the world due to Onassis' mammoth orders. When the *Olympic Cloud* (21,500) slid into the water on March 26, 1953, it was the largest tanker built by the Germans since the days of Hitler. Onassis was present at its launching and was feted for days afterward.

Niarchos also availed himself of the Germany ship-building efficiency and once again the two brothers-in-law attempted to go into business together. They wanted to buy a controlling interest in the Howaldtswerke's Kiel division ship-yards and when that was not feasible, they opted for a 49 percent purchase at the price of $6,500,000.

The proposition was fiercely opposed by the Social Democrats, who were in control of the municipality of Hamburg and who did not want any more foreign interference in their affairs than they already had. To discourage Onassis and Niarchos, without offending them to the extent of losing their business, the stipulation was made that if Onassis and Niarchos were permitted to acquire such a substantial amount of Howaldtswerke's stock, they would have to guarantee 100 percent employment for the entire shipyard for a period of ten years. To agree to such a demand would have been financial suicide, since the Korean shipping boom would most probably slacken — as it did — and the yard's production would eventually fall off consid-erably. Niarchos and Onassis appealed to Adenauer and made a counter-offer to construct a network of television stations throughout Germany, a communications system that the Germans wanted badly. Adenauer attempted to intercede in their behalf, but no compromise was possible. Both Onassis and Niarchos withdrew their bid and the matter was dropped.

Onassis continued building the largest tankers afloat, only to be temporarily bested by Niarchos' ships in a strange competition and a continuation of their fierce struggle that transcended mere urge for profits. Shortly, Onassis would be on top; their fighting continued for decades.

Onassis had a phenomenal memory. As he built more and more ships, his financial transactions were so complicated that his accountants often became confused about the details. Onassis kept all of the pertinent facts and figures in his head, however, and was able to spot the smallest error on one of his balance sheets. He did this all without notes and without any personal filing system. This mental ability plus his ability to do complicated mathematical problems in his head—he could long divide 437,321 by 847.21 for example—continually confounded and amazed his colleagues.

In July 1953, some 25,000 people crowded the banks of the Elbe River near Hamburg as the biggest merchant ship ever built, the *Tina Onassis*, (45,720 tons), at a cost of $65,500,000, slid into the waters after being christened by Onassis' daughter Christina, then two-and-a-half years old. Although notorious for paying low wages to seamen, Onassis ostentatiously announced that the captain of the *Tina Onassis* would be the highest paid merchant seaman in the world, with the exception of the commodore of the Cunard Line. "The world's largest ship," he stated, "had to have the world's best paid captain."

Not to be outdone, Niarchos launched the *World Glory* six months later, slightly less in tonnage (45,509 tons), but larger in the amount of cargo she could carry, (a capacity of 16,500,000 gallons compared to the *Tina Onassis'* 15,700,000), and therefore claiming the title of "The World's Largest Tanker." (The *World Glory,*after barely ten years of service, snapped in two and broke entirely apart during a storm and sank; sparks from the splintering vessel set off an explosion leaving nothing but refuse.) Niarchos followed that up with the 32,000-ton *World Justice*, the largest tanker ever built in Japan.

Onassis had still another ship under construction and less than a year after the launching of the *Tina Onassis*, the largest supertanker built to that day, the *Al Malik Saud* (King Saud I), slipped into the water at Hamburg amidst the cheers of over 100,000 spectators. The ship was so huge, so formidable and frightening looking (47,500 tons) that, perhaps for the first time in centuries, the term "she" with all that that implies, was dropped; she became "it." As a result of its size, it had a ghostlike quality to it. Because of automation ₐnd the simplicity of carrying oil as freight, its entire crew numbered less than 40 men, as opposed to the 1,285 officers and crew needed to man the *Queen Mary* which was comparable in size. It was really a beautiful ship, however, with graceful lines and modern touches. At sea,

87

whenever it was sighted by other ships, the *Al Malik* drew the attention of the sailors who would watch it with admiration as it passed their own vessel.

As Onassis and Niarchos continued in a competition to see who could build the largest tanker to realize the greatest profits, their contest became questionable, because if the tankers were too large, they would not be able to pass through the Panama or Suez canals. As it developed, through an accident of history, there was no need, temporarily at least, to design a ship that would have to go through at least one of these bodies of water. The Suez crisis was yet to come.

Onassis established the reputation of being the owner of the world's largest independent fleet of tankers. His only competition in numbers of ships were several U. S. oil companies. By the time the *Al Malik* was completed, he controlled over one hundred vessels with a carrying capacity under his house flag that totaled over 1,250,000 deadweight tons. Although Onassis strived to keep his financial affairs secret, much to the confusion of his competitors and also, possibly, to outwit the tax departments of several nations, it was estimated that in 1953 his assets totaled over $100 million. Some estimates ran much higher.

A certain awe and envy directed toward Onassis, not only by Greek shipowners but seemingly by the public of the country of Greece, began to emerge at that time. In a country as poor as Greece, this one man was making untold millions — his income was higher than the entire country's — and living a luxurious life that approached fantasy. Although the Greeks have always been seamen, the process of procuring ships before Onassis' time had been outrageously difficult. Traditionally, a group would buy a secondhand ship, so battered that Onassis' Montreal frigates seemed streamlined. Vessels were manned by friends and relatives, who were paid minimum wages. Safety precautions were practically nil. Some Greeks, who could still remember those spartan days at sea, resented Onassis' grandiose success and lifestyle and a feeling of umbrage developed toward him. It seemed not to bother him — outwardly, at least.

After having concluded one of the most famous

transportation deals ever transacted in the history of the oil business, Onassis named the *Al Malik* after King Saud I of Saudi Arabia as a gesture of goodwill and friendship and, as a token of respect to Saud's Moslem religion, christened it with holy water instead of the traditional champagne. Ultimately their agreement was broken and resulted in a $14 million lawsuit, and almost forced Onassis into total ruin.

Dealing with King Saud and his intermediaries in talks that were conducted over a period of one year, Onassis concluded an agreement, which was signed on January 20, 1954, that provided that he would get first right to carry all 42-million tons of petroleum and its products that the Arabian American Oil Co. (ARAMCO) produced annually in the Middle East. The proposition was made attractive since the charter company would be registered as a Middle Eastern concern and have its tankers fly the country's flag. At more than one of the periodic meetings of the Arab League, Arab leaders urged the creation or acquisition of national merchant navies. The only exception was that the Arabian American Oil Company (ARAMCO), or its parent companies, could carry oil in ships they owned and operated in the trade before December 31, 1953. ARAMCO was a consortium owned 30 percent by Jersey Standard; 30 percent by Cal Standard; 30 percent by Texaco and 10 percent by Mobil. Onassis was to set up the Saudi Arabia Maritime Co. (SAMCO) to run the ships he put into the trade. It would have its headquarters somewhere in Arabia. The Arabian government was to hold a controlling interest in the company and Onassis was to receive a substantial share of all profits made. When ARAMCO's ships eventually retired, Onassis' SAMCO tankers would take over, giving him an eventual monopoly on the transportation of most of the oil produced in the world, a business manipulation that would have meant hundreds of millions, if not billions of dollars of profit to Onassis over a relatively short period.

One of the important stipulations of the contract was that the estimated 40 million tons of oil to be shipped each year was to be carried at a rate higher than the normal market price. In return, Onassis agreed to pay a royalty of twenty-one cents on each ton of oil to the government for the exclusive right to carry the oil. In addition, he agreed to set up a fleet under the Arabian flag and establish a seamen's institute to train Arabian seamen in a long-term attempt by King Saud to bring self-sufficiency to his people.

What was not known at this time was that the Saudis thought that they might become embarrassed by supplying oil to the enemy if Onassis attempted to ship to Israel. A secret annex or amendment to the contract was therefore drawn up and signed by Onassis on April 7, which pledged that no Jew should have any interest "in any of these companies, directly or indirectly," and furthermore promised to boycott the Republic of Israel by stating "it is agreed the company will not deal with Israel."

Without even knowing about the secret amendment, the publicized deal brought immediate protests from several countries, including Britain, Norway, Denmark and Sweden who had been transporting most of the Saudi Arabian oil that was not carried in ARAMCO parent-company ships and eventually from ARAMCO itself, insisting that its own contracts with Saudi Arabia called for making oil available to everyone on a competitive basis. In England, the Chamber of Shipping attacked the agreement as "the gravest interference with normal commercial practices and flagrant flag discrimination." Although ARAMCO would still have the right to produce and sell the oil, they could see that eventually they might have to pay exorbitant shipping rates to Onassis' SAMCO. Shipowners, ARAMCO and other oil companies claimed that the Onassis contract would wreck free trade throughout the world. The U. S. State Department also condemned the Saudi-Onassis agreement, stating that it was a violation of international law. They believed it would eventually "give a virtual monopoly of all oil exports to companies controlled by Mr. Onassis." Later, they leaked the information that Onassis had approached four other countries in an attempt to establish the same deal with them — Iran, Iraq, Venezuela and the shiekdom of Kuwait, the leading oil producer at about 1 million barrels a day. Onassis denied it.

To add further damage to the reputation of Onassis, Niarchos gave a statement to the world press, wherein he said that the contract was a "political crime and economic monstrosity" and that he could understand why many of the countries in the world were condemning it.

Onassis had personal meetings with King Saud at the royal palace at Riyad and amended the contract in several ways. One paragraph was changed to read as follows:

"The company shall have priority in shipping and transporting petroleum products exported from Saudi Arabia by sea to foreign countries, whether the shipping is from Saudi ports or from the terminals of pipelines outside Saudi Arabia, and whether such shipping is carried out by the concessionaire companies themselves, their parent companies, or the off-taking companies."

This far-reaching clause would have had even further disastrous results to ARAMCO since it now comprised not only tanker-shipped oil, but all of Saudi Arabia's production of crude oil.

Onassis continued to push for the deal's acceptance because of a lag in the oil business and because the other oil companies he was dealing with were not committing themselves for long periods. Onassis' multiple ship construction was fast being completed, and he would have to provide business for them in a hurry or suffer a tremendous loss as some of his new ships went idle. He had 375,000 tons on order, with $35 million yet to be paid on the ships. Within a short while, those launchings, plus the ships he owned that were finishing their chartered periods, would have given him 500,000 idle tons in a less than dynamic market.

With the Saudi Arabian contract safely in his pocket, it appeared that Onassis had, in effect, defeated the oil companies. But they retaliated. No new contracts, from any of the oil companies that Onassis normally did business with, were forthcoming, and although the companies denied it, a genuine boycott was established against all of Onassis' ships.

Onassis fought back by doing everything possible to convince the oil companies that he was actually trying to aid the Saudi Arabians, and that his control of the oil shipping industry would be negligible, less than 10 percent of the total world tanker capacity.

He lavishly entertained the oil company executives at intimate dinner parties in his Sutton Square apartment, aboard some of his ships, at dinner at Maxim's in Paris, but it was to no avail. The companies would do nothing until the matter was settled between ARAMCO and Saudi Arabia. The dispute was taken to the international court at The Hague for arbitration, ARAMCO claiming Onassis' contract ran counter to its own 1933 agreement with Saudi Arabia.

To complicate matters, Onassis was sued for $14,210,000 by Spyridou Catapodis, a Greek shipbroker, who claimed that being retained and under contract to Onassis and working under his direction and approval, he paved the way to the ultimate completion of the contract with the Saudis.

Catapodis claimed that Onassis signed a contract that gave the former a substantial share of the profits from the Onassis-Saudi Arabian deal, ($14 million over a 30-year period). But after checking the contract almost a year later, Catapodis claimed the famous Onassis signature was no longer there, that in fact it had been signed by a highly volatile disappearing ink. He filed suits in Paris, Washington, D. C., and New York, but none ever went to court.

Onassis claimed that Catapodis was instrumental in cementing the agreement and that he promised him approximately $350,000 when the contract was signed, $210,000 when the first tanker sailed from an Arabian port under the agreement, 5 percent of SAMCO's profits and 2 percent commission on the gross freight carried.

Catapodis stated that he met with the Saudis, specifically Mohammed Alireza and his brother and Sheik Abdullah Hamdan, then Saudi Arabian Minister of Finance, and negotiated the details of the deal. Alireza asked for an outright payment of $1 million on the signing of the contract by the King, plus seven cents per ton of oil shipped, with a minimum of $168,000 a year. Catapodis alleged that when he relayed this information to Onassis, Onassis attempted to cut him and Alireza out of the deal completely by hiring Hjalmar Schacht, once Adolf Hitler's financial adviser who had long-standing and trusted connections with the Near East, to negotiate with Hamdan directly.

The Arabs became angry at Onassis' attempt to circumvent those considered to be "middlemen" and insisted he go through Catapodis and Alireza, the original negotiators. It was at this point, according to Catapodis, just before the King was to sign, that Catapodis was "astounded" to notice that his personal contract with Onassis had been signed with "invisible ink." When he confronted Onassis about the contract, Onassis admitted that the deal existed; Catapodis also had, in true cloak-and-dagger fashion, a witness, Leon Turrow, who testified that he had heard Onassis state that the terms of the deal were correct. Mr. Turrow was a former agent for the F.B.I. and a colonel during the war for the Criminal Investigation Department of the U. S. Army. However, all the courts that were appealed to would not accept the case on the grounds that it did not fall within their jurisdiction.

As ARAMCO and Saudi Arabia were attempting to negotiate and arbitrate, Onassis continued to try to persuade the oil companies to see his point of view, insisting that the Middle Eastern countries were, sooner or later, bound to set up their own tanker companies. He was quite open about the situation, perhaps overly so, when he gave this statement to Sydney Mirkin of the New York *Daily News*.

"They stuck to drilling, exploitation and marketing. When they made these oil agreements, transportation was not considered as a major item. As things turned out, particularly after the war, transportation became important and profit-making."

With the new amendments to the contract guaranteeing Onassis all the oil from Saudi Arabia, ARAMCO was not the only company due to lose millions. Niarchos alone estimated a multi-million dollar loss and was determined to do something about it. Through a friend of Catapodis', Niarchos had heard that the $1 million "bribe" had actually been offered by Onassis to Mohammed Alireza, to secure the contract, and if Niarchos could prove and publicize that fact, he had a chance

93

to undermine the contract. He had his attorney, calling from London, make contact with Robert A. Maheu, at that time a private detective, later to become an aide to Howard Hughes and a participant in various plots initiated by the C.I.A. to kill Cuban Premier Fidel Castro.

Maheu was hired by Niarchos to "make sure that no oil was ever shipped under the contract" and to "sabotage" it in any way that he could. Further, he was told to concentrate on trying to determine whether the $1 million bribe offer was true, and if so, he was requested to secure evidence to prove it as a catalyst to undermining the deal.

The first thing Maheu did was to secure a copy of the contract itself. When he realized that Onassis would be controlling more deadweight tonnage than the United States itself, and that it would have greatly affected the economy of the country, he briefed both the National Security Council and the C.I.A., and received their support and cooperation in his attempt to scuttle the contract.

Working with C.I.A. agents in Rome, Athens, Saudi Arabia and New York, Maheu established surveillance and investigation teams. He had a listening device secretly placed "for a few days" in a light fixture in Onassis' suite at the Hotel Pierre in New York. Eventually, he became convinced that the $1 million bribe had been made, but he was never able to find tangible proof of it.

At the request of the C.I.A., Maheu attempted to leak the stories to several newspapers in Rome and elsewhere in Europe, but was unsuccessful in his attempt since he could not substantiate his accusations, even though he knew all the details. However, Maheu was able to persuade *Ethnos*, a newspaper in Athens, to publish the story of the $1 million offer. Shortly after the paper appeared, King Saud announced his intention to compromise with ARAMCO, dropping the Onassis contract in its entirety.

Even though it appeared that Onassis lost out on the greatest financial manipulation of his career, it is possible that the entire Saudi Arabian-Onassis contract was done as a maneuver on Onassis' part to goad ARAMCO into granting him a larger share of long-term tanker contracts than it had in the past.

Later, in a more humble tone, he admitted he had made a colossal mistake:

"I made one great mistake. I never thought that in our world emotions could override all business reason. For almost a year, I had reports that Saudi Arabia was looking for someone to provide it with a fleet to carry its surplus oil. I knew that certain parties were out to get the contract.

"I sat and watched and it was like watching a loaded gun lying around there, which anyone could grab. Finally, I became convinced that somebody was about to make the deal and rather than let it go to competitors I went for it myself.

"And landed in the biggest mess of my life.

"My intention was 95 percent defensive," he added. "But when I went to the people to whom I owed so much [presumably ARAMCO], who had helped me in the past, they would not listen to me. They threw me out.

"They got emotional, their attitude was, 'Here is a man we fed, whom we helped to grow' (which is quite true) 'and the dirty heel turns around and shows his ingratitude!'

"Why, it's exactly the same as an employee who makes a move, learns that his boss is mad at him, goes to the boss to explain his reasons and before he has the time to open his mouth his boss yells at him 'You are a disloyal so and so. Get the hell out of here' — and the employee has no chance to explain what he meant."

Despite the humility of the statement, Onassis, however, continued on the offensive, and in a short while he was threatening a countersuit against ARAMCO, citing the U. S. Anti-Trust Laws, and stating that if he lost the two billion dollars he believed he would have made if the deal had been consummated, he would sue ARAMCO for the full amount.

In some ways, the Saudi Arabian-ARAMCO oil conflict was the nadir of Onassis' career. Later, boycotted by the oil companies, more and more of his ships became idle and this was costing several hundred thousand dollars each week, to say nothing of the anticipated profits he lost.

The only relief he received came in the spring of 1955, when the Socony-Vacuum Oil Co., one of the four American firms owning ARAMCO, made a surprise call to Onassis saying that it wanted to charter the *Al Malik*, and that it agreed to have the ship sail under the Saudi flag.

On the surface, the charter appeared to be a victory for Onassis, but as it turned out, his position hardly improved. The giant ship was substituted for two Onassis tankers under charter to Socony, and in the final analysis, the *Al Malik* carried less oil than the two tankers combined, thereby creating a further cut to Onassis' profit. In addition, Onassis had offered the *Al Malik* for charter with other smaller tankers on the New York ship market in order to begin to prove his anti-trust case against ARAMCO. The chartering of the *Al Malik* by Socony immediately demolished that case. There seemed little Onassis could do to extradite himself. In what seemed like a last resort, he began negotiations with Royal Dutch Shell to sell them his complete million-ton tanker fleet; the price offered by them, however, was more than 30 million less than Onassis was willing to consider and the negotiations died aborning.

Then, through an incredible historical coincidence, almost overnight, Onassis' fortunes suddenly turned dramatically and profitably around again. Facing almost certain ruin because of the oil boycott, Onassis soon made more money in a shorter period than he had ever made in his life. The catalyst was the Suez Canal.

In the summer of 1956, Egypt's President, Gamal Abdel Nasser, nationalized the Suez Canal, barring Israel from its use. In retaliation, Israel invaded the Gaza Strip and the Sinai Peninsula with the backing of English and French troops. The U.S. and the United Nations appealed to the Israelis to withdraw when Russia threatened a nuclear attack against the West if the fighting against Egypt, its ally, did not cease. In the interim, Nasser not only closed the Suez Canal to all traffic but totally immobilized it with sunken ships.

Immediately, oil from the Near East, supplying

Europe and the United States took much longer to transport. The oil tankers were forced to go all the way around the continent of Africa to reach the North Atlantic. The possibility of limited oil supplies threatened the reconstruction of Europe. Britain imported 65 percent of its oil through the Suez Canal and France, 45 percent. While the Suez was closed, most European countries bought their desperately needed oil supplies from the United States and South America but the rates were much higher—almost more than the war-ravaged countries could afford.

As a result of the Suez situation, it took more than twice as many ships and twelve additional days each way to transport the oil from the Near East. Onassis had many extra ships, not under contract, that could be leased to handle the demand. Because his ships were not contracted, he possessed the power to charge whatever rates he could get, and as the cry for more oil was heard, the price for transporting rose as quickly as a skyrocket—from less than $4 a ton, Onassis was soon charging over $60 and each tanker-full from Arabia to Europe was earning him a profit of over $2 million a trip. For a while, heads of countries considered Onassis to be so involved with the Suez crises that he was acting as though he were a government in himself, receiving calls, giving advice, quoting prices, meeting with foreign investors, issuing statements to the press. By the time the Suez Canal was opened again, in April 1957, it is estimated that Onassis realized a profit of over several hundred million dollars. Onassis took no credit for his unprecedented success, "I was lucky" was his only comment.

"Like most wealthy people, he has very few friends. There were a whole lot of people who were just hangers-on, and others who were merely there to profit from him in every manner.

"For whatever the reason, suddenly Onassis changed from his original enthusiastic attitude towards Monaco to a manner I found quite strange. All at once, I discovered, there was no longer any dialogue possible with him. I mean by this that you could speak to him for an hour, two hours, three hours, but when he went out of your office you knew perfectly well that nothing of what you had talked about was going to be followed through."

His Serene Highness, Rainier III
Sovereign Prince of Monaco

In the spring of 1951, Onassis with his 21-year-old wife, Tina, rented one of the most fabulous homes in Europe, the Château de la Croë, located on 25 acres in the south of France at Cap d'Antibes between Nice and Cannes. It had formerly been the home of the Duke and Duchess of Windsor.

Before moving into the house, he hired a staff and a "manager" to take charge of his household affairs, feeling that Tina was too young and inexperienced to successfully cope with the responsibility of so large and grand a house as Château de la Croë. She wrote at that time in an article that appeared in the *London Daily Mail*, that she was "totally unambitious . . . everything happened to me so soon and so young." They had two small children, Alexander and Christina, and Onassis thought caring for them should be Tina's main concern. There were over two dozen servants, which included gardeners, maids, cooks, chauffeurs, butlers and dishwashers.

When Tina was finally shown the house, she could hardly believe the sumptuousness of it; even though her father was one of the richest men in the world, the Château de la Croë went beyond her fantasies. She clapped her hands and laughed when she was taken to their apartment, deep within the Château, and shown her private bathroom. The size of a large living room, it had the feeling of an Egyptian bath, was beautifully mirrored; the bathtub itself shaped like a huge white swan, with accessories all plated in gold. Everything was framed by a majestic black marble floor.

Two huge salons had a glass roof that could be opened electrically and Tina often sunbathed inside her own home while watching the children play.

The Château had magnificent grounds, manicured lawns, numerous fountains and a swimming pool, and the property ran directly down to the sea. The children had a variety of pets — a Great Dane, two French poodles, a horse, a goose and two gazelles (which were a gift from King Saud of Arabia). Onassis loved to spend time with Alexander, and even though the boy was only three, Onassis taught him to swim in the pool. Within a year, he was also giving him informal lessons in Greek, and the child learned the language with great speed.

Onassis received some personal notoriety on the Riviera soon after moving into the Château. Not only were his neighbors interested in what kind of man could afford one of the most splendid homes in all of Europe, but they became curious at his strange method of water-skiing. Instead of being towed by the conventional motorboat, he would hitch his line to the back of a seaplane and go roaring through the water at great speeds — at times even being lifted into flight — much to the awe of the onlookers on shore.

It was an idyllic life, and Onassis thought that he would remain there for many years. Hardly a week went by without a lavish party being given by the Onassis', to honor such stars as Lili Pons, Claudette Colbert, Merle Oberon, Gene Tierney and Greta Garbo. Although Onassis had met Garbo when they were neighbors at the Ritz Tower Hotel in New York, at that time he rarely spoke to her other than to say "good morning" at the elevator. It was not until he moved to the French Riviera, that they became friendly. Garbo had been vacationing there for years and they began attending the same parties. Actually, their first lengthy conversation took place at a party in England at J. Paul Getty's baronial mansion, Sutton Place, where the usually uncommunicative Garbo was charmed and entranced by Onassis to the degree that she talked to him for hours. Pulitzer Prize winning journalist Fred Sparks, in one of his accounts of their relationship, wrote of that first night, "For the first time that any of those present could recall, Garbo came bursting out of her shell, and after dinner she sang Swedish folk songs, and, solo, did several Scandinavian dances; then calling for a bathing suit, she jumped into the pool . . . ." Onassis had a strange effect on Garbo. He possessed an intimate knowledge of her career and a genuine liking for her. She respected him and was touched by his interest in her. Norman Zierold, one of her biographers, said that "Garbo was very gay in Onassis' presence. At one Monte Carlo club she sang to the accompaniment of violins. The melody was a Greek song, "Saapair," whose title translates to mean, 'I love you.' "

For years after that, Garbo and Onassis spent time together on his yacht and she was his guest many times at the

100

Château de la Croë and at his other homes throughout the world. They both were relaxed with each other, and there are photographs of the two of them together where she is beaming, obviously happy to be with him. Occasionally, however, Onassis would overdo his hospitality. Once when meeting her at the Nice airport, he had a brass band accompany him! Garbo was horrified at the crowds that the band attracted and refused to get off the plane until they dispersed. She did not think his prank was very funny. Another time, she almost jumped overboard when he invited some newsmen and photographers aboard his yacht. He was forced to send them back to land, via motor launch, without any of them ever setting foot on the ship.

Garbo would usually make a discreet exit whenever any other woman entered Onassis' life. What was stranger, however, was that in all the years that they knew each other, they never became lovers. Only once, after he had had too much to drink, did Onassis suggest the possibility of a physical relationship, at least for the evening. "Go to sleep, Ari. Don't ruin our friendship," Garbo told him. Onassis obeyed and that was the end of the beginning.

Although Tina was young, beautiful, educated and had a love of life — seemingly everything Onassis might want in a wife — he began spending time away from the Château, and not only on business. In retaliation for being left alone, Tina herself would go off to the luxury of St. Moritz to ski — a sport that Onassis detested. She also inherited her father's penchant for thrift and was appalled at the way Onassis parted with his money. They argued constantly about it. She was aware of the age difference between them and it annoyed her that they seemed to have little to talk about. He often referred to her and Alexander and Christina as "my three children," while she was known to call him "the old one." Eventually, although there was no mention or hint of divorce, they built separate sets of friends that each spent more and more time with. Hers were drawn from a group of young skiers at St. Moritz; his from a varied group of shipowners and international celebrities in all of the cities where he did business. Tina fell in love with

101

Renaldo Herrera, scion of one of the wealthiest families in Venezuela, and she was seen dining and dancing with him in cities throughout the world, over a period of years. Onassis knew of Tina's relationship but did or said nothing, since he himself was unfaithful, having affairs, from almost the first months of the marriage, with a number of women. After their first year of marriage, he spent less than 90 days a year living with Tina, but they nevertheless kept up "appearances" and decided to stay together, because of their children. Despite their differences and apparent disregard for each other, they still loved each other. Onassis was Tina's first love, in every sense of the word, and from the very first time that they became serious about each other, he felt protective and loving toward her, elevating her to the status of a Greek goddess of sorts — a very inexperienced goddess, but a goddess nevertheless.

Although he had offices in New York, London, Paris and Buenos Aires, Onassis wanted additional commercial and working space nearer his new house, and hence, the following encounter with the fairy-tale land of Monaco.

The episode began when Onassis decided to rent some office space as close to the Château de la Croë as he could. He loved the climate and enjoyed his neighbors, which included Martine Carol, a French actress, and Catapodis, at that time a good friend. Niarchos, too, lived nearby. Onassis found that commuting between Paris (home of his business operations) and the Mediterranean took too much of his valuable time. He needed an office closer to his arena of business, since much of his tanker business consisted of transporting oil from the Middle East through the Mediterranean to Northern Europe. The miniature principality of Monaco, half the size of Central Park, was the perfect spot for his operations center. It was much closer than Paris to Marseilles and Genoa where many of his ships were repaired, and the tax advantages were extremely seductive. There were no individual or corporate income taxes in this tiny postage-stamp country by the sea.

In 1952, Onassis attempted to lease for his company, Olympic Maritime, the Winter Sporting Club of Monte Carlo, a spacious building owned and operated by the Societé anonyme des Bains de mer et du Cercle des Etrangers (Sea-Bathing Society and Foreigners' Circle, Inc., of Monte Carlo). At that time, the S.B.M. was having severe financial difficulties. Gone were the days when Alexandra, Czarina of Russia, brought the entire company of the Imperial Ballet to dance when she gambled, or when kings, queens, princes and princesses, earls and dukes, gambled away half their kingdoms and still laughed over it. New stock transactions and reorganization of the S.B.M. board became commonplace. It seemed like a ripe time for Onassis to step in and save the financially ailing club. When he offered to rent the Sporting Club on a long-term basis, the S.B.M. board turned him down. Onassis did not fit the conservative image of the S.B.M. members.

Onassis would not accept the snub and was so infuriated he decided "to do something else." Like a Walter Mitty come to life, his idea of "something else" was to buy the entire S.B.M. corporation. This company owned the 75-year-old Monte Carlo Casino, the Hotel de Paris—one of the world's finest—three other hotels, the only theater in Monte Carlo, the golf course at Montagel and other choice real estate, including, of course, the Sporting Club. But first, before he could make the purchase, he had to become friendly with the right people. Among the right people were Prince Rainier III and his girl friend Gisele Pascal, a beautiful French actress. Gisele had a profound effect on Rainier. Like Ari, the Prince and his girl friend loved the ocean, and at the time of Onassis' S.B.M. projections, they were looking for a yacht to cruise the Mediterranean's turquoise waters. Onassis found the perfect pleasure ship for the couple—a 137-foot diesel-powered yacht, the *Deo Juvante II* for a "bargain" of 51 million francs or roughly $120,000.

While Onassis was courting the Prince, who enjoyed his flamboyance, his brokers in the Paris Bourse were purchasing every available share of S.B.M. stock from any of its 31,000 stockholders who were willing to sell. Much of the stock was purchased quietly and under false names, so the S.B.M. was unaware of what was happening. At first, the principality, jealous of its sovereignty, denied that Onassis had any more than 2 percent of the stock, but at the annual meeting of the stockholders, the truth came out. Onassis eventually bought about one third of the shares of S.B.M. stock. With the consent of Prince Rainier, himself a 20 percent stockholder in S.B.M., Onassis bought the entire S.B.M. in January 1953. The deal included possession of Monte Carlo's biggest real estate corporation with $20 million in assets. Onassis' first business decision was to fire the entire board of directors who had refused to rent him the Sporting Club. He then moved in a 100-man staff, and remodeled the offices at a cost of $100,000. He also quickly invested $2.5 million to add four floors of apartments to the venerable Hotel de Paris and subsequently moved into a six-room penthouse at the top of the structure.

Until he became "the man who bought the bank at Monte Carlo," Onassis was hardly known by the general public, and those who did know the name, simply thought of him as a rich Greek shipowner. After his purchase of the S.B.M. stock, like Byron, he awoke one morning to find himself famous. Full-blown celebrity had descended upon him. "Once Penniless Man Buys Control of Monte Carlo Casinos," stated a headline in *The New York Times*, and from that day (Jan. 16, 1953) on, Onassis had to live with a constantly relentless corps of journalists and photographers who followed him everywhere. Soon reporters from all over the world began to track him down and interviews and profiles of Onassis began to appear in Sunday feature supplements of newspapers everywhere. He felt he needed a public relations agent to "handle" his image. Some of the articles that were appearing weren't all that favorable and Onassis was afraid that adverse publicity would negatively affect his shipping interests. He hired Nigel Nielson, a bright New Zealander, who was based in London. Onassis asked Nielson to meet with him at Monte Carlo and asked him to come prepared with what Nielson discerned was the public's true feelings about who Onassis was. When Nielson began to mention such Onassis idiosyncrasies as his aversion to the press, his profligate parties aboard the *Christina*, his untold millions garnered somewhat unscrupulously, Onassis stopped him before he could go any farther. "I'll tell you what the public thinks of me" contradicted Onassis, "they think of me as a Greek with too much money." Nielson was instructed to demolish that attitude and he began by inviting a number of well-known writers and reporters to come to do stories, true ones, of what Onassis was really about. In a short while, the tide began to turn and favorable articles, usually in the British press, where Nielson had most of his contacts, began to appear, using such descriptive adjectives as "brilliant," "charming," and "friendly"! Onassis' desire to "correct" his image became so pronounced that some time later he even accepted an invitation to be on a special television program and interviewed by David Frost. He never did appear, however.

Onassis also hired John W. Meyer as a public relations aide. Meyer was formerly with Warner Bros. in Hollywood and for a number of years worked for Howard Hughes. He received national attention, after the war, during the Senate investigations of Hughes' participation in the National Defense program. Meyer was asked to substantiate the amount of $169,666.17 spent over a period of four years on Hughes' behalf. As it developed, much of this money was used as expenses in entertaining some of the most beautiful women in Hollywood in *their* entertainment of aircraft manufacturers.

Onassis was impressed by Meyers' uninhibited aplomb and soon "stole" him from Hughes. Thus, Meyer began a career as a general factotum to Onassis, a position that lasted a lifetime and included handling invitations to the *Christina*, buying Onassis' favorite cigars and spending countless evenings with him in the nightclubs of the world. Their relationship transcended that of employer-employee and Onassis considered him a true friend. Meyer also gave Onassis important advice about Howard Hughes' assets. Late in 1954, Onassis formed a consortium consisting of himself, Laurance Rockefeller and William Zeckendorf, the real estate operator, in an attempt to buy and gain control of Hughes' vast industrial empire. Through his old friend Spyros Skouras, Onassis had learned that Hughes was toying with the idea of divesting himself of all his holdings with the exception of RKO Studios. Zeckendorf was appointed negotiator for the group, and with

Meyer's help, a secret appraisal was made of the various corporations. Ultimately, the three men made an offer of $400 million for the Hughes Tool Co., Hughes Aircraft, Hughes' brewery in Houston and a number of his other allied interests.

Zeckendorf was in phone contact with Hughes daily and eventually Hughes also talked with Onassis and Rockefeller before he came to a decision. He told Zeckendorf that in principle he would accept the offer. Zeckendorf checked once again with Onassis and Rockefeller to secure their commitment and was off to Hollywood the next day, contract in hand, ready for Hughes' signature. Upon arrival in California, Hughes did see Zeckendorf but in 24 hours' time had mysteriously changed his mind. "I never agreed, nor had any intention of selling anything to you," he told Zeckendorf without further explanation or rationale. The matter was dropped.

When Ari purchased the S.B.M., Monte Carlo was much too drab for his tastes. He decided to give the entire country a face-lift, starting with the Sporting Club. Monte Carlo would be a playland, once again, for the rich and powerful. Onassis wanted to build skyscrapers, reclaim part of the sea for recreational use, and add restaurants and recreational facilities for a variety of sporting events. He criticized the formal Monte Carlo Casino for its stuffiness and had it redecorated. He also promoted major cultural events. Soon orchestras, ballets, and other theatrical troupes were booked for Monte Carlo performances.

But no sooner had Onassis begun to renovate and reorganize the tourist industry in Monte Carlo, then the country was hit with a financial disaster — the bank failed.

Constantin Liambey, a friend of Onassis and financial adviser to Prince Rainier, persuaded the Prince to invest most of his money in a series of commercial deals. The advice proved to be faulty. In July 1955, Rainier almost went bankrupt. His monetary depression, however, was soon over. Rainier announced his engagement to Grace Kelly, who some people thought was the most beautiful woman in the world, and within an hour of the announcement, Onassis donated 1 million francs to a pet royal charity. They were married on

April 18, 1956, amidst a rainfall of red and white carnations (Rainier's family colors) from Onassis' seaplane.

In her book, *The Dream Boats*, Nancy Holmes writes about Onassis and the Rainier marriage by quoting columnist Mrs. Bob Considine, who, along with fellow journalist Art Buchwald, was invited aboard the *Christina*.

"We had just arrived for the wedding week, and it was early morning when we ran into Ari in the bar at the Hotel de Paris. He invited us to lunch on *Christina* and the moment we got aboard we went over to the deck on the port side, and we watched as Prince Rainier steamed out on his tiny yacht, *Deo Juvante*, to fetch his bride-to-be from the S.S. *Constitution*. Since we were the only guests aboard, and it would be some time before Rainier came back with his future princess, Ari took the time to give us a tour of *Christina*. He loved showing her off. The suites were fantastically large and the paintings were all priceless. The bar was really king-sized, and interested Art Buchwald and me the most, not just for the drinking. Ari told us that the bar stools, which looked as if they were covered with drum heads, were actually covered with the foreskin of a whale's penis. That alone gave Buchwald and me fodder for conversation for some time to come.

"A few nights later, Art was seated at a dinner party next to Betsy Drake, who was married to Cary Grant at the time and seemed like a prim, proper and remote girl. Thinking it would shock Betsy out of her cool, Art told her about the bar stools covered with the foreskin of a whale's penis. Betsy looked nonplussed for a moment, and then she exclaimed, 'Oh, Moby's Dick!' *That* broke some ice.

"But back to that first day. We all had caviar and some *ouzo*, the milky licorice-tasting Greek drink that Ari favored. When Rainier sailed back from the *Constitution* with Grace, who was wearing a ridiculous big white organdy hat that she had to clutch constantly to keep it from blowing away, we leaned over the side of *Christina* and looked down; and believe me, from the *Christina* we had to look way down at *Deo Juvante*. The entire harbor was bedlam, with cannons booming, planes and helicopters circling and fluttering around, and fireworks exploding overhead throwing out thousands of small Monagasque flags. We bombarded the happy pair from *Christina*, with pink and white carnations shot out of special small cannons, floating down in little parachutes. The Prince was beaming and waving. Grace was hanging onto her hat for dear life. It was *quite* a day.

"During that week of festivities preceding the Royal wedding, we all ended up every night at a nightclub in the Casino where we joined Ari. We drank more champagne than I ever knew existed. At about four A.M., when the Casino closed, Ari would walk across the plaza like a Pied Piper, with the orchestra and those of us who had lasted still following along with him, all singing at the top of our lungs. We'd stop at the Cafe de Paris for breakfast and dance on the sidewalk while the orchestra played for us and everyone who cared to join us. Then, he would take us back aboard *Christina*, music, strangers and all, and we would dance and play until dawn. It was fiesta time, and as far as most of us were concerned Onassis was top banana, not Rainier."

Onassis was responsible for giving the royal couple a lavish wedding reception at the Sporting Club and, as an additional gift, gave them a Bemelmans painting and to Princess Grace, a diamond necklace.

New attention was focused on Monte Carlo after the wedding and many Americans began shifting their businesses to the tiny principality. It had the first mini-boom in years and Onassis was making money.

On occasion, the prima ballerina, Dame Margot Fonteyn, and her husband, Tito Arias, an expert in international maritime law, would cruise the Mediterranean with Onassis on the *Christina*. Arias conferred and talked business with Onassis while Dame Margot rested, sunned and socialized. In her autobiography, she paints a vivid portrait of her host:

"Onassis had extraordinary charm and was a perfect host, always relaxed and unhurried. I thought he lived in a very intelligent and civilized manner. His preferred hour for discussing business was about two in the morning, so Tito sometimes slept for a couple of hours after dinner in order to have a fresh mind later on. As Onassis never went to the theater or ballet, I was surprised to find he knew a bit about entrechats-six. He said he had greatly admired Pavlova when he was a very young man in Buenos Aires and his eye had been caught by one of the dancers in the company."

A young American promoter, Martin Dale, was interested in attracting American investors to Monaco. With the "go ahead" from the Prince and his wife, Dale established the Monaco Economic Development Corporation (MEDC). Now money began to pour into Monagasque banks as it had been doing for years into Lichtenstein. In a short period, over two thousand foreign firms were listed in the Monaco Trade Register, most for tax purposes. Nevertheless, industrialization did take place and new apartment buildings began to sprout up all over the country. Sparked by General Charles de Gaulle, competing businessmen in neighboring France began complaining about the tax-free status of business in Monaco. De Gaulle considered the tax dodge as a surreptitious method by foreign countries to enter the Common Market; he rejected Great Britain, and he certainly rejected businesses from such countries as Lebanon and Morocco who were being sheltered by Monaco. The French government soon intervened and compromise taxes were paid by Monaco's business community.

Onassis and Princess Grace and Prince Rainier had quite different ideas about the development of Monaco. Ari wanted the country to remain a playground for the jet set. Princess Grace, on the other hand, wanted Monte Carlo to be Europe's new cultural center. The Princess had things her way.

Prince Rainier and Onassis became great social friends, though they had many business disagreements about the future of Monaco. To celebrate their fifth wedding anniversary, in July of 1961, the Rainiers joined Onassis, Maria Callas, Elsa Maxwell and several other friends on a cruise aboard the *Christina* to Palma de Majorca. The group stayed

109

at the San Vita Hotel where the Rainiers had spent their honeymoon and on July 15, the night of the anniversary, had a huge party that lasted until dawn and boasted an unusual musical—Maria Callas played the caracas, Prince Rainier the drums, Elsa Maxwell the piano, Aristotle Onassis and Princess Grace sang.

The Onassis-controlled S.B.M. had grandiose plans for the urbanization and development of Monaco. Rainier, although in favor of these plans, felt that progress was much too slow. He and Onassis argued constantly about this. Rainier accused Onassis of abandoning his financial responsibilities to Monaco and blamed this lack of interest on Ari's failing marriage. By then, there were rumors that he might be going to divorce Tina to marry opera diva Maria Callas. He was always in her company.

Also, much to the ire and embarrassment of Rainier, newspapers were beginning to refer to Onassis as "Monte Carlo's Uncrowned King" and made constant references to the fact that the *Christina* dwarfed the *Deo Juvante*.

In the final months of 1959, there was discussion by people connected with the Paris stock market that Onassis was trying to buy up all the S.B.M. stock available. The price per share more than doubled from $4 to $9. Onassis was already in control of the S.B.M. and the speculation was probably started by rumor.

A mammoth and almost comic-opera dispute, as beclouded as their relationship (that eventually went to court), began again between Onassis and Niarchos over the S.B.M. stock transaction. Onassis claimed that he "allowed" his brother-in-law to buy $150,000 worth of S.B.M. stocks so that he could be assured of office space, like Onassis, in Monte Carlo. Niarchos claimed that he gave Onassis two checks totaling $250,000 which were to cover a 50 percent controlling interest in S.B.M. After the court determined that the amount exchanged was $250,000, and that since the time that Niarchos had given him that check, the price of the stock had gone up considerably, it was determined that Onassis owed Niarchos $400,000; but that upon payment of this sum, Onassis would own the stock outright and Niarchos would not be considered a partner. Onassis was not satisfied with the court's decision, however, claiming that $100,000 of the money paid to him by Niarchos was for a seaplane that he had sold to him; $8,000 he advanced for a wedding gift he bought for Niarchos for one of the latter's employees and $16,000 he advanced for salaries for Niarchos' employees when his funds were tied up. To confuse matters even more, Niarchos stated that he owed Onassis $45,000 for a DC-3 they bought together, but that the seaplane money was paid by a separate check. Eventually, the dispute was arbitrated, Onassis paid Niarchos $132,428 and kept the stock, while Niarchos retained the seaplane. Despite their difficulties, they continued their partnership in the DC-3.

Onassis began to respect the Prince's wishes and built a Sea Club, a new indoor swimming pool and a new bowling alley. The Scottish Club was also constructed. While the Prince was delighted with his new facilities, Onassis was upset about this large outlay of capital. The new urbanization plan would tear down some of the recently constructed facilities in a few years. Onassis' investments would be wasted.

Although Onassis was in financial control of the S.B.M., Rainier had the power to veto all appointments of S.B.M. officials. The veto power was written into the country's constitution and Rainier was not at all timid about exercising his control. At Rainier's whim, the leadership of the S.B.M. was removed and replaced several times during his association with Onassis. Onassis was trapped, impotent. He owned the S.B.M., but could not effectively control it. The corporation had far too many employees, but Onassis could do nothing about thinning out the staff. The employees were registered voters in Monaco. Rainier had to keep his principality pacified.

Rainier wanted new hotels, new sporting clubs, new apartment buildings — to the tune of a $10 million investment. He demanded that Onassis issue a couple of million new shares of S.B.M. stock to raise the necessary money. Onassis said that the money could be found if Rainier relinquished his veto power in the S.B.M. The Paris Bourse would not permit a capital increase of more than 30 percent of its current worth.

Rainier was angry and talked about nationalizing the S.B.M. Rainier's plan did not go through.

In 1965, Rainier complained in *Le Monde* that Onassis and the S.B.M. were ignoring Monaco's interests and were only interested in profit-making ventures. The S.B.M. counterattacked by charging that Rainier had sabotaged the company's activities by administrative inaction. In between the accusations, Onassis and the Prince continued to socialize. In the summer of 1966, they shared a table at Europe's most fashionable charity ball, the Bal des Petit Lits Blanco, the most lavish social occasion of the year in Monte Carlo. White linen runners covered narrow streets converging on the fifteenth-century palace of the Grimaldis. There, in the cobblestone square fitted out with a dance floor, footmen with powdered wigs and red livery held flaming candelabra, fountains flowed with whiskey and champagne, and 48 lambs, skewered with swords, rotated slowly over sputtering coals. To the music of eight orchestras, Prince Rainier danced with Maria Callas, while Onassis danced with Princess Grace. Outwardly, all was calm but the schism was near.

Onassis talked about building middle-class apartments in Monte Carlo for vacationers from all parts of Europe. Princess Grace stated,

"Monaco is one place that has kept a nineteenth-century charm. I hope that never disappears . . . I don't think Monte Carlo can ever be a place for mass tourism. It has always been glamorous, always for the rich. It's not so much for increasing our number of tourists. It's more for modernizing a conception of what people look for on their vacations . . . Monte Carlo has always had a lot to offer. But people need to be reminded. We all tend to fall asleep here in the sun."

The quarrels continued. Onassis later announced that gambling should be banned in Monte Carlo. "It's immoral," he said. Rainier was incensed, "Really, Mr. Onassis, I don't think you are in a position to tell me what is moral or immoral," obviously referring to the open love affairs of Onassis. Rainier asked Onassis to sell his shares in the S.B.M. because Ari was obviously not interested in the future of Monaco. Onassis rejected many proposals including one in which the Banque de Paris would restructure the S.B.M. into three corporations.

Rainier used the French-owned Monte Carlo radio station to deliver a blistering attack on Onassis. Without mentioning his name but referring to the S.B.M., Rainier asked: "How can we plan a tourist policy without alluding to those who draw great profits?" He then talked of "their constant shiftiness which badly disguises, under false pretexts, the absence of all desire for collaboration with the government."

Finally, in 1967, the National Council of Monaco passed a law forcing the S.B.M. to issue 600,000 new shares of stock with a market value of $8 million. The law instructed the S.B.M. to buy out Onassis at $16 a share. Onassis protested, stating the shares were worth at least $50 each. He appealed the decision to the Monaco Supreme Court. Onassis lost the case and on March 17, 1967, the Monaco Treasury paid Onassis $10 million for his S.B.M. shares. Onassis was outraged about the decision, "We were gypped," he told the press.

Onassis' personal and business friendship with Rainier and his Hollywood wife was soon terminated.

Onassis and his guests arrived at dawn in the Antarctic Ocean by amphibious plane. They were accustomed to jetting at will to the ski slopes or sandy beaches. For their amusement, he had flown them instead to the land of the icebergs.

The great factory ship *Olympic Challenger* was near two whale catchers, which had just returned with two huge blue whales, both over 90 feet long. The carcass of one whale still hung on one of the catchers, forcing the boat to list slightly. The water for hundreds of yards around the ship was red with the dead whale's blood.

The other whale lay steaming on the deck of the *Challenger*, waiting to be butchered.

Standing on the bridge deck, Onassis explained to his friends the details of the process. No one averted his/her eyes. Using long knives to peel off the blubber, 175 men, all experienced craftsmen, began to work synchronously. The blubber was pushed down into hatches and the boiling began, until the fat was turned into oil. Everything else was cut, sliced or diced, and then preserved—the meat, the internal organs, the bones, even the teeth for scrimshaw carvings. The tongue alone weighed over three tons. The entire 150-ton whale was butchered in exactly one hour.

The cold was bitter, wet, piercing. A steward brought a tray of glasses filled with brandy. Onassis spoke to him in German and he answered deferentially. Everyone drank the brandy rapidly, then the steward led the guests to their staterooms to rest. Onassis stayed atop, mesmerized by the activity below him, continuing to concentrate and supervise with his eyes.

Although Onassis truly believed that casino gambling at Monte Carlo was "immoral," he was not averse to taking other gambles, much greater than could be won or lost in a single night's wagering. "My whole life has been a terrific gamble," he once said and probably no other venture that he participated in was more imbued with risks and unpredictable vagaries than his experiences in the whaling business.

Whaling has been, by tradition and circumstance, one of the most chancy and competitive businesses in the world, dominated throughout history by the United States, Scandinavia and Germany with little opportunity for an outsider to learn or become successful in capturing the great leviathans—each a fortune afloat—or doing so on a consistently profitable schedule.

Onassis was the first Greek seaman ever to become seriously involved in the pursuit of whales, incited by his love of ships and the sea and by the enormous stakes that could be won through a prosperous business.

During the post-war shipbuilding period, Onassis was approached by the owners of the First German Whaling Co., who suggested a joint partnership to establish a new and dynamic whaling enterprise. Although he was warned by his financial advisors not to take the risk and tamper with what was already the largest shipping concern in the world, he decided to go ahead. He once explained exactly why he chose to go into whaling, "Well, of course, you can make a lot of money in it. But apart from that, something intangible about it seemed to attract me. In the first place, it's a hell of a business to learn. I suppose, looking back, it was an answer to a challenge."

Onassis' previous experiment in whaling on the coast of California gave him hardly enough experience to manage a multi-million dollar whaling operation, but he had ships and capital, which were what the Germans lacked at that time, while they had veteran crews and the proficiency of decades of hunting whales. It was a totally equal partnership.

Onassis established the Olympic Whaling Co., registered it in Panama, and quickly went about building a whaling fleet. He bought a former American tanker and appended the name *Olympic* to it—the first time he used the word on one of his ships—to be used as the factory ship and employed a flotilla of Canadian navy ships as catchers. The Canadian frigates had been purchased earlier by Onassis with the idea of converting them into passenger ships to cruise the Greek islands. He could not gain the necessary financial cooperation he needed from the Greek government, however, and ultimately abandoned the plan, temporarily placing the ships in "mothballs." All were eventually reconverted as whalers at the Howaldtswerke at Kiel and on October 20, 1950, set out to Antarctica on their first expedition.

Already under large amounts of pressure from contracts to furnish whale oil for the production of margarine, Onassis entered upon one of the blackest areas of his financial career, a story of wholesale slaughter unparalleled before or since in the history of whaling. Violating the regulations of the International Whaling Commission, whose laws were established in order to keep the dwindling herds of certain species of whale from becoming extinct, Onassis' whalers, from their very first expedition, started to hunt well before the season officially opened, continued after it had ended, strayed outside of the confined hunting areas and killed a huge number of noneligible whales, such as cows and calves or those below the regulated minimum size. His whaling fleet was also the first in history to use helicopters as spotters, and although not illegal, seemed highly unfair and unethical at the time.

In order to continue the hunt without being detected after the end of the season, the captain of the *Olympic Challenger*, the mother ship, ordered radio silence. The funnels and names of all the ships were camouflaged so that they could not be identified, and all ships were ordered to hide behind icebergs as soon as another ship, however distant, was spotted.

The crews of Onassis' ships were outraged over the flagrant disregard of the regulations and on several occasions were near mutiny. A protest was filed by the crew and given to the captain and the expedition chief. It said, in part:

"We Germans would not want to have it said of us that we did not abide by the whaling convention, for this could readily be turned into an argument against allowing Germany to ever have another whaling fleet of its own."

His first year of whaling was, under the circumstances, enormously profitable. His expenses ran about $1 million and the industry average profit for that expense usually ran from about $800 thousand to $1 million. Onassis made a net profit of $8.5 million during his first year. Onassis sent out another expedition to Antarctica in the winter of 1951 and 1952 which was also profitable, but because of a drop in whale oil prices, did not send his fleet in the 1953-54 season.

By then Onassis' tactics as an unscrupulous whaler had become well known throughout the industry and at the International Whaling Commission meeting in Tokyo in June of 1954, the news that Onassis was returning to the whaling arena in the next season caused a communal trauma and an outcry from the participating countries. It was charged that he was rapidly depleting the entire whale population by the killing of cows; eventually, perhaps in one or two generations, it was argued, the entire whale population would be wiped out. Onassis had to be controlled, it was demanded. Onassis was called an "international outlaw," but until such time as facts could be collected proving his unethical practices, it would be impossible to stop his fleet from hunting.

Onassis defended himself, of course, blaming the Norwegians and stating that the allegations hurled on him were untrue:

"I have been attacked from the moment I have entered whaling. Everything was done to make the project impossible and the source of all the accusations was Norway. We had no complaints from the British or other expeditions. Right from the beginning, the Norwegians were out to get me. The first thing they did was to call up the shipyard in Kiel and give warnings that if they worked for me they would be boycotted in Norway. But by that time the contracts had been signed and work had begun. It is a fact that when I realized the opposition, I was willing to get out and let Norway carry the contracts. Perhaps I got cold feet. But Norway would not do this. They would not find the currency. Then they warned that any Norwegian joining my fleet would have his passport withdrawn and his property in Norway confiscated. Wives of Norwegians who joined me were spat at in the streets as though they were the wives of Quislings. It got so bad that some had to leave the country and live in South Africa, Chile and elsewhere. Big oil buyers were canvassed not to buy oil from my expeditions."

Britain, however, *did* know of his unethical practices and as the second largest whaling nation, actually offered to give — completely free — Onassis 4,000 tons of whale oil a year, for four years, if he withdrew from the industry. Although he would have realized a profit of over $2 million, for doing absolutely nothing and taking no risks, he refused, believing that he could make greater profits as the price of whale oil continued to rise.

It was in this atmosphere of condemnation that Onassis became involved in what has been described as his own personal one-man war with Peru.

When the Olympic Whaling Company began an expedition for sperm whales off the coast of Peru in August 1954, the Peruvian press branded Onassis a "whaling pirate."

118

Headlines attacked the Onassis expedition: PIRATE WHAL-ING FLEET DEFIES OUR NAVY appeared as the front-page headline of *La Prensa* on August 24.

The press reported that the Onassis whaling fleet, led by the massive *Olympic Challenger*, did not only not comply with any of the International Whaling Commission regulations, but that Onassis had violated Peru's national sovereignty by whaling within a 200-mile limit set by the Peruvian government. (The 200-mile limit was discussed in Santiago, Chile, in August 1952, when Peru, Chile and Ecuador decided to establish 200-mile wide national "waterways" off their boundaries. These nations voted to prosecute any trespasser of their "waterways" and fine them accordingly.) An article in *Nacion* in August 1954, read in part, "Pirate invasions as practiced by Onassis cannot be tolerated. If they do occur, the trespassers must be apprehended and their vessels seized by our Navy." Onassis thought that the 200-mile limit was preposterous, arguing that the sea was free and that outside of the three-mile limit agreed upon for years all over the world, his ships could go about their business and do as they please; he considered any interference from any coastal government a war-like act.

His whaling business was to him, a "terrific gamble," in any event. He said of it, "I have one thousand men in that fleet and it costs me more than $35,000 a day to operate it. You gamble against the elements—storms, fogs, icebergs. You gamble that you will find whales. And suppose everything goes well, and in six months you bring back a good cargo of oil. Then comes the biggest gamble of all. Prices of whale oil you can never predict. Maybe I will get $11 million return on what I laid out, maybe I will get only $3 million and I will lose a million or two."

Because most of the crew members of the Onassis fleet were German, tempers ran high when news reached the German press. "The Peruvians would not dare stop the *Olympic Challenger*," huffed the Hamburg press. "The Peruvians are bluffing."

The Peruvians were not bluffing. President Manuel Odvia was infuriated with Onassis and had no intention of allowing him to "rape Peru." On November 15, 1954, Peru became the aggressor. As two of the Onassis ships, the *Olympic Lightning* and the *Olympic Victor*, were spotted whaling about 180 miles from the Peruvian shore, two Peruvian destroyers, the *Aguirre* and the *Rodriguez*, ordered the whalers to surrender for trespassing in Peruvian waters. The ships were taken to the port of Paita. On the same day, another Peruvian ship, the *Castilla*, and several other destroyers captured two additional ships of the Onassis fleet. The crew members were arrested and questioned by Peruvian police.

The next morning, the mother ship, *Olympic Challenger*, under the command of Reichert, was actually attacked by the Peruvian Air Force. According to two Panamanian whaling inspectors who were aboard the *Challenger*, the ship was 380 miles from the South American coast. As warning bombs were dropped around the ship, Captain Reichert ordered the chief engineer to move full speed away from the Peruvian coast. One bomb ripped a hole in the ship's side and machinegun fire riddled the deck. No one was killed or injured but the intent was clear. The *Olympic Challenger* surrendered to the Peruvians.

Although spokesmen for the Onassis fleet stated that the ships were well outside the 200-mile limit imposed by Peru, the Peruvian Government announced officially that all the other whalers had indeed been captured within the 200-mile territorial limit. In the days following the *Challenger* capture, two other catchers of the Onassis fleet, the *Olympic Conqueror* and the *Olympic Fighter,* surrendered to the Peruvians. At least six of the Onassis ships, however, escaped the Peruvians and entered the port of Balboa, Panama.

Onassis was in London when he first heard of the plight of his fleet. Publicly, he was decidedly and surprisingly cool. "We're waiting to see what will be done," he said. Privately, he considered sending a convoy of his own ships, fully armed, to blast the Peruvians out of the water. Sarcastically, he added that if the Peruvians can expand their territorial limit from 3 to 200 miles, then the United States might as well broaden its limits "a couple of thousand miles and include

Australia among its territorial possessions." Onassis told British reporters that his fleet entered Peruvian waters because the President of Peru had promised the President of Panama that his fleet could operate 50 miles off the Peruvian coast. Since the Onassis fleet was flying under the flag of the Panamanian government, Onassis telephoned officials in Panama and instructed them to take proper diplomatic action against Peru. The complaint, however, coupled with proposed protests to the United Nations and the Organization of American States, failed to resolve any of Onassis' problems. He soon transferred the flag of his fleet from Panama to that of his adopted homeland Argentina.

In Germany, news of the capture and attack of the *Challenger* outraged the press. A banner headline in the *Bild-Zeitung* of Hamburg read BOMBS ON HAMBURG SEAMEN: OUR SAILORS TREATED AS FAIR GAME. Families of the crew members demanded information about the safety of their loved ones. Fears were silenced on November 22, when the Onassis Agency in Hamburg received a wire from Captain Reichert: "All restrictions on crew aboard ship as well as on land lifted . . . our men . . . all in good health . . . sending regards to relatives."

When the Peruvian investigators searched the impounded *Challenger*, the ship's log indicated that almost 3,000 whales were caught off the Peruvian coast. Within two weeks of the fleet's capture, the Peruvian Naval Court had fined the Olympic Whaling Company $3 million. If the fine were not paid immediately, Peru threatened to incorporate the Onassis ships into the Peruvian Navy. Onassis laughed at this threat, labeling it a "Peruvian pipe dream."

Germany had already protested the actions of the Peruvians and the British government was soon to follow with support of the Onassis whaling expedition, stating that Peru had no legal right to prevent whalers from sailing off the Peruvian coast. The British commended Onassis for testing the validity of the Peruvian 200-mile limit.

Britain's interest in the whaling adventure ran much deeper than the legal issue of territorial rights. Onassis, with

121

his special brand of business acumen, had purchased a $14 million insurance contract with Lloyds of London to cover every conceivable disaster that a whaling fleet could possibly come up against. The Lloyds' insurance policy included a highly controversial "war risk" provision, as well as $30,000 per day in payments up to a maximum of $900,000 if the fleet were detained through confiscation. The policy also covered all fines. Onassis, it turned out, would not be financially responsible for the fines imposed by the Peruvian court; the money would have to come from the British underwriters. And each day his ships were out of action, Onassis was $30,000 richer.

Debates livened the usually somber insurance business throughout the world. Why would Lloyds of London offer such a comprehensive policy to Onassis in the face of the Peruvian government's public announcements preventing whaling ships from entering its waters? While Lloyds' financial reasons might have been sound, their political motivations for issuing the policy were based on a logical, if wrongly calculated, assumption that Peru was too weak a nation to stage war on a whaling fleet, especially one flying under the flag of Panama, a close political friend of the United States.

The British government asked for and was granted two extensions to obtain the $3 million demanded by the Peruvian court. Finally, on December 11, Charles Dixon, the Lloyds' representative in Peru received instructions from the London office to pay the fine.

There appears to have been conflicting reports of where the $3 million came from for payment of the fine. While the money was supposed to be provided by Lloyds of London, the money may actually have come from Onassis himself and later have been reimbursed by the London firm.

On Monday, December 13, Mr. Dixon, Don Roberto Aleman, an Onassis representative, and a high official from the Peruvian Ministry of Finance met to complete the payment of the fine. The money had been sent to Lima from the National City Bank of New York. The Onassis representative paid the assessed fine to the Peruvian official, but not without

122

making a formal protest to the Peruvian Government. Mr. Aleman was granted permission to appeal the fine to a higher court. The Panamanian Government announced that payment of the fine did not mean that Peru's territorial limit was sacred. Peru, however, felt assured that payment of the fine brought credence to its 200-mile "waterway" sovereignty.

After the fine was paid, Onassis had only one concern — to get his fleet to the Antarctic in time for the whaling season beginning the first week in January. He offered his sailors an extra month's salary as an incentive to reach the southern destination before January 7. Onassis, operating from Jiddah, Saudi Arabia, relayed this information to his Panamanian managers in a private code.

Immediately after receiving the message, the *Olympic Splendor*, a 30,000-ton tanker, left Balboa, Panama, with a fleet of 12 catchers to rendezvous with the *Olympic Challenger* and the ships released from Peruvian captivity. The fleet was soon to join 19 whaling expeditions from around the world for the Antarctic whaling contest.

In the United States, there was considerable discussion about the Peru-Onassis confrontation. Traditionally, policymakers held the view that the seas could not be owned and should be free to all nations. A country has no legal right to extend its water limits. Others, however, felt that Onassis' private and commercial ventures were becoming too monopolistic and threatened American interests, especially his oil transactions in the Mideast. The Americans' resentment of Onassis eventually caused the American government to accept Peru's 200-mile sovereignty.

The United States' acceptance of Peru's policy caused tensions around the world. Britain, Norway and other countries with an important whaling economy were adamant in their support of Onassis and his right to fish in Peruvian waters. Both economically and politically, Onassis was clearly the victor in the Peruvian "whaling pirate" incident.

A strange footnote to the incident was that the *Aguirre* and the *Rodriguez*, the Peruvian ships which seized two Onassis ships on November 15, 1954, were originally sold to Peru by Onassis himself shortly after World War II.

At the end of the 1955 season, Onassis sold his whalers to Japan for $8.5 million and withdrew from the whaling business altogether, with the following comment, "On the whole, we did fairly well but it was nothing in comparison to the risks we took. I have sometimes thought I shouldn't have done it. Anyway I *have* done it. And now I'm out of it. It's one hell of an experience you don't forget!"

It was in his private quarters on the *Christina*, out to sea late at night, when everyone else was asleep, that Onassis had some of his best moments. Usually working bare-chested in bathing trunks or slacks and sneakers, he would pace back and forth in his cabin for hours, pausing briefly at his desk, staring down at it—but really at nothing in particular —and then continue his pacing, thinking through the intricacies of his business operations.

He loved the loneliness of working far into the night, for somehow he felt less alone during that time than when he was with people. The slight hum of the ship's engines kept him company; the moon and starlight shining in his windows kept him alert. He had trained himself to need very little sleep.

His secretary, Jenny Rocca-Serra, whose cabin was directly beneath his, said that not only could she hear

Onassis move about at night, but she thought she could almost hear him think. In the throes of business creation, his mind worked not like a precision watch but like a forceful engine, finely tuned, and with great power.

On some evenings, he dealt with oceans of specifics, giving his protean attention to the details of his corporations—making five, ten, twenty transatlantic calls, issuing directives, solving very real financial conundrums.

Occasionally, he would walk the deck, in fair weather or foul, sometimes for hours, and lose himself in the complexities of his thoughts. Most of the time, he was not really conscious of his reasoning or thought processes, except that they usually involved a struggle and ultimate conquest of himself. He was a man of instinct, and by the time the dawn began to light the interior of his cabin, he would have come to the conclusion—whatever it may have been—that he was seeking.

When Constantine Karamanlis was elected as the new premier of Greece in 1957, he vowed to attack and solve the poverty-level economy of his country. One of the ideas he had was to initiate the construction of a new shipyard and expand and modernize in every way T.A.E., the Greek National Airline, for years an ineffectual and profitless operation which was close to bankruptcy.

Karamanlis approached Onassis to see if he would be interested in investing and taking over the control of either venture. Onassis showed immediate enthusiasm about both operations. The shipyard would be an enormous investment but had special tax advantages and Onassis was eager to diversify his investments. The airline, which consisted of just seven planes, serviced only some of the larger cities and islands of Greece, with the exception of one flight each week to London and Paris. Onassis assumed, correctly, that there might be great financial possibilities in establishing an international run from Athens to New York and to other parts of the world, as well. The airline owned landing rights in New York City.

Onassis submitted bids to the government on both projects and waited for them to be accepted. What he did not know was that Stavros Niarchos had appealed to Queen Frederica to have Greece accept his bid over Onassis' for both the airline and the shipyard.

There was an attempt by the government to get both men bidding against each other with the possibility of larger and larger investments. This worked to a degree, until such time as the amounts of money to be involved were getting too large. For a period, it appeared that both Niarchos and Onassis might abandon the projects entirely.

At the same time, Karamanlis was being pressured by the Queen and Onassis. He attempted to negotiate a compromise by suggesting that both men form a joint partnership and operate both businesses equally. Neither would even consider such a proposition.

Eventually, a compromise was worked out whereby Onassis purchased the commission to the airline for twenty years and Niarchos had the right to build the shipyard. Onassis insisted that Niarchos pay the same amount for the shipyard that he had offered and the latter agreed. It is my belief, based on interviews, that the Greek royal family was financially involved with Niarchos in building the yard. That might explain why Queen Frederica so avidly lobbied for her friend.

Onassis' first step in reorganizing the airline was to rename it Olympic Airways. He added new equipment, new planes, new offices and about $15 million as an initial investment. By 1963, he began to show a profit.

Because he enjoyed building something from nothing, as he had done in his youth, and because of the "glamour" of the airline business, Onassis delighted in his purchase and the fact that he was in control of the world's largest personally-owned airline. He took a special and immediate interest in the airline, which transcended his life-long involvement with ships. Although he followed the movements of his tankers from the *Christina* by an occasional telex directed to one of his various homes or offices, he was constantly involved with most of the details, even quite small ones — on a daily basis — of *Olympic*. His managing director once described Onassis' interest in the airline, "He's thrilled by it." Onassis even went so far as naming both Monte Carlo and Olympic as his "hobbies," with the implication that both ventures made up just a small portion of his total financial interests and income.

In 1965, Onassis attempted to get a $30 million government loan to buy three Boeing 707's. He believed the time had come for Olympic to inaugurate transatlantic service. It looked as though the loan would go through, until the Papandreou government fell and was taken over by the Greek colonels. Instead, Boeing itself issued the credit to Onassis, and at Paris' Orly Airport, in 1966, Onassis snipped a ceremonial ribbon at the boarding ramp of a blue and white Boeing 707 jet, starting transatlantic service for his airline. In addition to the routine conveniences of in-flight motion pictures and nine-channel stereo, Onassis' planes featured stewardesses in uniforms designed by Chanel, dinners from his favorite New York restaurant, "21", and complimentary champagne. Having fought for ten years to bring his airline to the point of "respectability," Onassis did not offer spartan service to its customers.

Later, it was revealed that Andreas Papandreou had no intention of granting the loan because Onassis had asked for a guaranteed rate of return on his investment, with the further stipulation that the government would have to prevent any airline strikes at any time in the future. The proposal infuriated Papandreou who became further incensed when Onassis made an offer to "contribute" $1 million to Papandreou's Center Union party. Onassis was ordered out of Papandreou's office and told not to return.

Even though Onassis had luxurious owner's quarters built into all of his ships for his own use, he had always dreamed of a flagship entirely his own, a vessel that could operate as home and office, get him to or away from any corner of the globe, and serve as the true microcosm of his own personal universe.

With this in mind, one of the Canadian frigates, the *Stormont*, purchased for $34,000 for his whaling operation, was kept for his own personal use. This ship, which was built in 1943 and had served as an escort to convoys in the Atlantic during the war, was totally reconverted into one of the most modern, most elaborate and most expensive private yachts ever built. Keeping only the hull, the shipbuilders at Kiel painstakingly constructed and outfitted a new ship which was to serve as his base of operations, a floating Xanadu.

He named the ship *Christina* after his daughter, and by the time it made its maiden voyage in June of 1954, he had spent over $4 million in redecorating and reforming her.

Christina is a sleek 325 feet long, spotlessly, almost religiously white, and weighs 1,450 tons, with a large canary-yellow funnel. It flies the Liberian flag and can obtain a speed of 18 knots, 22 in emergencies. It takes five to six hours to prepare the boat for sailing, but on a number of occasions, when Onassis was in a particular hurry, it was done in less than two.

An open, spacious lounge at the stern is covered with a green canopy. At the center of this area is a mosaic reproduction of a fresco from ancient Crete. The mosaic is used as a dance floor in the evenings and during good weather days, as the dining area. It is framed by a large border in gilded bronze. With small white tables and chairs set up, it resembles and has the charm of an outdoor cafe or a small European plaza. At the push of a button, within 50 seconds the mosaic floor is lowered nine feet and the entire area forms a full-sized swimming pool. At night, a system of water fountains with colored lights plays on the water in the pool, all in the same colors as the mosaic.

The open lounge section enhances the lines of the original frigate, with its graceful canoe-like, ice-breaker stern, and is the favorite spot on the ship for Onassis and most of his guests. As an article in the *New York Times* described the outdoor lounge, "Here are such teak decks, flawless varnished woodwork and polished brass as have been rarely seen since the passing of J. P. Morgan."

Off the open lounge, reached through sliding doors finished in antiqued Japanese lacquer, is a large living room or salon, called the Game Room. Measuring 35 feet by 20 feet, it has the feeling of a nineteenth century parlor handsomely paneled in oak with a heavily beamed ceiling. A grand piano is at one end of the room and a wood-burning fireplace at the other. The facade of the fireplace is covered in deep blue gemstones and is guarded by two bronze lions from the Yuan dynasty. The floors are covered with thick Turkish rugs woven in Onassis' birthplace, Smyrna. It was in this room where his guests usually met and congregated.

Flanking the fireplace are shelves with books in English, French and Greek (with leather bands along the shelves to prevent them from falling during a rough sea) on a number of subjects, predominantly murder mysteries and ancient Greek history. The collection contains some scholarly and historical works, such as Sir Arthur Evans' treatise on the excavation of the palace of Knossos on Crete and the complete works of Winston Churchill, given to Onassis as a gift from the author. Excepting some of the works of Greek history and mythology, it is doubtful whether Onassis read many — or any — of the books on his shelves. He was thoroughly schooled in Greek mythology, however, and would often quote lines from Homer, with particular reference to Ulysses, his favorite tale. However, according to his associates, he was never seen reading a book and if he displayed knowledge of a popular novel, for example, it was always a superficial acquaintance with it, garnered from the press or a chance remark he had picked up in conversation. He was a voracious reader, however, of magazines and newspapers and was usually *au courant* about what was happening in the world. The *International Herald Tribune* was delivered to him every day wherever he was, and he read everything in it from the front page to the last.

Above the fireplace was a strangely poor painting of Onassis' daughter, Christina, and on other walls were paintings of Alexander and Tina, in addition to a small portrait of a youth by El Greco titled "The Charcoal Burner," curiously hung in a dark corner where it is difficult to see and appreciate.

Off the Game Room is a small area with a circular bar. Its glass top sets over a lighted replica of the sea, with tiny models showing the development of ships and shipping throughout history. The ships can be moved by magnets. Among these ships is a tiny wicker basket, which flies a flag inscribed "Moses — the first shipowner." The bar was stocked with almost anything that anyone would care to drink, and the wine cellar in the hold of the ship contained a mammoth collection of some of the world's best vintages.

Polished whales' teeth, collected by Onassis' whaling fleet, were turned into footrests on the bar stools, and as hand-holds on the rim of the bar for use when the ship rolled. The bar stools were covered with the foreskin of a whale. "You are sitting on the world's largest penis!" Onassis would say naughtily, and usually to women, and wait for their reaction. The teeth on the bar were ornately carved with scenes from a series of paintings depicting Ulysses' return from Troy which hang in the Munich Museum.

The ship had literally hundreds of ship models, many of them carved in ivory and exhibited in shadow boxes set into the bulkheads. Most of the models are of the French ships from Napoleon's fleet. They were made by French sailors who were captured when the fleet was defeated in 1810, and who whiled and whittled away their jail sentences in English prisons by fashioning models of the proud ships they'd sailed.

There is an elaborate stereo system with a large collection of both tapes and records. If music is played during the day, it is usually "light pop," and in the evenings "classical," anything from Beethoven to Vivaldi.

Off the bar is a large, bright area known as the Children's Room, decorated with murals of Parisian fantasy scenes by Ludwig Bemelmans, Onassis' friend from Hollywood. Tiny bright yellow tables and chairs were used for dining by the Onassis children, but by the time Alexander reached the age of 11 and Christina 9, they ate in the officer's mess room.

On the same level and down a long, wide corridor, "protected" by two huge bronze mythological falcon-like birds, were the guests' quarters. There were nine individual suites, each containing a bedroom, living room and bath and affording luxury comfort. Each was named for a different Greek island — Lesbos, Corfu, Ithaca, Rhodes, Andros, Crete, Chios, Santorin and Mykonos — and each cabin suite was designed and furnished by a different artist. On the door of each suite appears a medallion in gold leaf in the shape of the island, below it, the name given in English and above it in Greek. All are air-conditioned and soundproof.

There was also a small hospital aboard, with x-ray and surgical equipment, an operating room and a special autonomous electrical system that will go into effect if the ship's electrical system becomes defective. A doctor was always in attendance on every trip that lasted more than one day.

Perhaps one of the most unusual, non-nautical features of the *Christina* was the corridor outside the lounge; it contained a splendidly graceful spiral staircase. During the day, with the bright sunlight streaming in through the windows and playing around the marble banisters, it took on the appearance of the entrance hall of an elegant Mediterranean villa, rather than the inside of a ship. The staircase led to a smallish, circular dining room with murals by Marcel Vertes and to a reception hall where the major parties were held, large enough to accommodate over 200 guests and a full dance band.

The journalist Joachim Joesten relates this story about the murals of the dining room, "When the interior of the *Christina* was nearing completion, Onassis commissioned a French painter, Marcel Vertes, to do four large oils. The artist chose the four seasons as his theme.

" 'Spring' showed Onassis' two young children, Alexander and Christina, frolicking on a flower-studded lawn; 'Summer,' the *Christina* riding at anchor in Monte Carlo Harbor; 'Fall,' Mrs. Tina Onassis sitting in a garden, alone and forlorn, with yellow leaves falling; and 'Winter,' a grimy, dejected beggar huddling in his rags on a snow-covered bank in New York's Central Park.

"Shortly afterwards, I visited the *Christina* in the harbor of Monte Carlo. I was especially eager to see the pictures. Except for 'Spring,' they weren't what I had expected; 'Summer' showed a bathing belle on the Riviera; 'Fall,' Tina Onassis swinging gaily in a hammock, and 'Winter,' a pretty ice-skater whirling about. The story I have been told on good authority is that Onassis had seen his own features in the pinched face of the beggar and thereupon ordered Vertes to

132

supply a new, and more pleasing set of pictures." New paintings were supplied and although the subject matter was changed, the quality of the paintings was not. They are one of the few truly hideous decorations on the entire yacht.

The formal silver used for dinner and special luncheons was designed by Tetard, a famous Parisian silversmith, under the direct specifications of Onassis. It is inspired by utensils used in ancient Crete. The china is white and gold Bavarian porcelain, with the gold medallion of Greece in the center. The glassware is Baccarat crystal with a twisted stem and a flag of the *Christina* engraved on the base.

At a cost of thousands, Onassis had flown to the *Christina*, almost daily, French bread from Paris and a certain type of orange which grew near his villa at Glyfada.

Off the dining room and reception hall were several lounges, including a motion picture theatre. One flight up, Onassis' personal quarters and office, a suite which someone once described as an ideal sitting room for Lorenzo the Magnificent, ran the full width of the bridge deck. Oak paneled, with a Louis XIV desk, the room was decorated with a pair of gold sabers given to him by King Saud, Turkish dueling pistols, armor of various countries, and Onassis' favorite painting—another El Greco, this one of the Virgin Mary and child, which Onassis purchased at a cost of $200,000. There is a rumor that the painting was a reproduction, and that Onassis kept the original safely in a vault. Supposedly, no insurance company would insure such a valuable work if placed in a location in which it could easily be ruined by the sea air. Definitely not a reproduction was a green jade statue of Buddha, studded with rubies, made by the jeweler of the czar and one of three existing in the world (the second is still in Russia, the third in Buckingham Palace). Onassis' cream and sea-green bedroom, the largest on the yacht, was decorated with authentic Venetian furniture, and spread around the room was a collection of more Greek, Russian and Byzantine icons. Charmingly, there was one straight-back wooden chair in the room, given to Onassis by his daughter. Crudely carved on the back is, "With my love and many kisses, Christina."

Onassis' private bathroom is perhaps the most beautiful room on the boat. Done in marble from Siena, it is an exact copy of the bath of King Minos in ancient Crete. The bathtub is blue, white and gold mosaic. The faucets, in the shape of dolphins are all gold plated, and cost more than the price of some small yachts. They are exact copies of the faucets in the master bathroom of the Château de la Croë. Like the bathtubs on the *Queen Mary*, it is possible to fill the tub with four different types of water — hot fresh, cold fresh, hot salt and cold salt. Off the bathroom is a large dressing room with a wall to wall and floor to ceiling mirror, a sofa and a dressing table.

One curious addition, a perfect example of Onassis' sometimes bizarre and voyeuristic personality, is the door from the study to the bathroom which consists of a two-way mirror. When Onassis was enthroned inside, he could see anything that was going on in his office, without anyone being able to see him. Once Onassis was greatly embarrassed when a workman, in repairing the door, replaced the two-way, see-through mirror in the wrong direction. During a formal business meeting, Onassis excused himself and used the bathroom. Sitting there in silence, he looked up to observe his associates in the other room and was aghast when he realized they were staring back at him in disbelief!

It was in his private study that Onassis spent a great deal of time, mostly at night after his guests had gone to sleep, making transatlantic telephone calls to his various companies and keeping his multifaceted empire together. The radar and ship-to-shore telephone operation which allowed him to operate with perfect ease, even while aboard ship, was one of the most sophisticated systems ever installed in a private yacht. There were 42 extension phones aboard, many of them hidden away in the drawers of tables. Once, while cruising the Aegean, he claimed to his guests that he could be connected to anywhere in the world in a matter of minutes. One of his guests looked skeptical. "Give me a number," Onassis demanded, and the guest gave his mother's phone number in Washington, D.C. Onassis picked up the receiver, dialed the international prefix and area code and the telephone number, and handed the receiver to the guest, who stuttered a surprised hello to his mother, more than 7,000 miles away. The electrical power that is used for the yacht supposedly could light an entire city with a population of 10,000.

In case the telephone should ever prove insufficient to his need to communicate at high speed, Onassis kept aboard ship a small white Fiat with cane-covered seats, an Italian amphibious seaplane with a range of 1,200 miles, four Chris-Crafts, a hydrofoil speedboat capable of a speed of 60 miles per hour, two smaller speedboats, an auxiliary sloop of six tons, complete with wireless and complete galley and refrigerator, and two lifeboats, all of which could be lifted off and onto the deck by a huge, self-contained crane. It sometimes made the deck of the *Christina* look like the set of a James Bond movie. For sporting purposes, there are also two kayaks, one of which was often used by Onassis himself, who, in order to keep in shape, oared for an hour or more a day when he had the time. He also swam about 50 laps a day in the ship's pool and walked about one or two miles each day around the decks.

In overall length, the *Christina* is about the same size as the old U.S. Presidential yacht, the *Mayflower*, and just slightly smaller than J. P. Morgan's famous yacht, *Corsair*. According to Lloyds' Register of Yachts, the *Christina*, when it was completed, was the sixth largest yacht in the world, only surpassed by Britain's royal *Brittania*, the United Arab Republic's *Al Houria*, the late Raphael Trujillo's *Angelita*, and Saudi Arabia's *Mansour* — all owned by heads of state. The *Moineau*, owned by Mrs. Lurienne Benitez Rexach of the Dominican Republic, is the largest personally owned yacht in the world. Although there are yachts larger than the *Christina*, outside of Cleopatra's barge, with its deck of beaten gold, silver oars and perfumed sails, there has never been a yacht quite as luxurious as Onassis' ship.

In addition to its decadently splendid trappings, the *Christina* was equipped with the most modern safety devices of any ship constructed. An electronic control board in the wheelhouse indicated whenever a porthole was opened, and if the temperature of any part of the ship rose above normal, an automatic fire alarm was activated. Two pairs of stabilizers kept the ship roll-free except in the heaviest of storms. The latest British radar and high-precision navigation gear were standard equipment.

From the time of its maiden voyage and for the remainder of his life, Onassis spent more time on the *Christina* than in any of his houses, apartments, or villas spread throughout the world. Being on the sea, in control of wherever he wanted to go, his privacy intact if he so wanted it, enabled him to be the captain of his own directives—to feel totally independent.

But the *Christina* did more than provide Onassis with his separate universe. For Onassis, it was truly his home. Tina once said that to her husband the yacht "was not a fantastic plaything but a real passion. He is almost like a housewife fussing over it, constantly looking to see that everything is being done well, constantly looking for things to correct and improve." Because it was of the sea, the *Christina* was undoubtedly Onassis' most cherished possession, an example and symbol of his wants and desires. Once, when asked where of all of his houses he preferred to live, he snapped: "The *Christina*, of course!"

At first, the entire crew was German but Onassis kept replacing them over the years, one by one, with Greek seamen from his tanker fleet. Each new crew member was handpicked by Onassis after being carefully interviewed by him. They all had to be precise and experienced at their work, reasonably attractive, speak at least one language other than Greek and be excellent dancers, the skill to be used, if necessary, for any of the companionless female guests who might be aboard for a cruise. In addition to the sailing crew, there were stewards, maids, bartenders, chefs, laundresses and a governess for a total personnel count of 65. The crew worked together so perfectly, whether it was serving a formal dinner or docking the yacht, that they rarely had to speak to each other, communicating with complicated but subtle gestures of their eyes.

As the yacht was his home, Onassis used it as the focal point for his entertaining. Through it, he expressed his natural Greek hospitality. Parties aboard the *Christina* were among the most lavish and celebrity-studded of any in contemporary society, certainly any upon the sea; not to have gone up the gangplank of the *Christina* to at least one party, produced in the mind of the jet-setter "the kind of inferiority complex that enriched a psychiatrist's couch" according to international society columnist Lanfranco Rasponi. For large parties, Onassis had entertainment flown to the yacht—everything including an entire string orchestra from Paris, to a group of *bouzouki* players from Athens, some flamenco dancers from Seville—all to delight such renowned guests as Douglas Fairbanks, Jr., Cary Grant, John F. Kennedy, Greta Garbo, Winston Churchill, Marlene Dietrich, Elizabeth Taylor and Richard Burton, Princess Margaret, Gregory Peck, King Farouk, Tito Arias, Frank Sinatra, Konrad Adenauer, Cole Porter, Bernard Baruch, Adlai Stevenson, Ava Gardner, Dame Margot Fonteyn, and of course, Maria Callas and Prince Rainier and his wife, Princess Grace. These names represent just a few of the hundreds of celebrities who spent time being entertained by Onassis, and he hosted everything from formal dinner parties to cruises that were weeks long. An invitation to the *Christina* became a status symbol even for the very famous, and Onassis had an almost constant round of guests wherever in the world he happened to be sailing.

There were some occasions when the number of guests were strictly limited, however, and that was whenever Winston Churchill and his wife were aboard. In Monte Carlo in 1957, Onassis was interviewed by Churchill's son Randolph for an article he was writing for an American Sunday newspaper supplement. Onassis remarked that he had always admired Randolph's father and would consider it an honor to meet him one day. Churchill was vacationing in Monte Carlo at the time, and Randolph mentioned Onassis' comment to his father, who consented to a meeting. He said he had been fascinated by Onassis and had always wanted to meet the famous Greek shipping magnate. Within a few days, Onassis invited the Churchills, senior and junior, to lunch at the Hotel de Paris in Monte Carlo, and thus began a long and extremely close relationship. The day after the luncheon, Churchill wrote, in a letter to his private secretary, "I met a man yesterday called Onassis. He is a man of mark."

To many, the closeness between Onassis and Sir Winston was difficult, if not impossible, to understand. Churchill, undeniably one of the greatest public figures of the twentieth century and one of its best educated and most brilliant, was a statesman and leader of the highest order. First minister to the King of England, a Nobel Prize winner not only for literature but for oratory as well, Churchill was one of the world's grand old men, revered not only by the British but throughout every Western country. What did he have in common with Aristotle Socrates Onassis, admittedly one of the world's richest men, but also a man who had been indicted and found guilty by the U.S. Justice Department, a business tycoon who used somewhat unethical practices to amass his fortune, and a man who had carved out a reputation as a consummate playboy?

The answer is not a simple one, but clearly from that first lunch until his death in 1965, Churchill was a close friend of Onassis. He spent every vacation with him, and enormously enjoyed his company. Once, when asked why he spent so much time on Onassis' yacht, he answered, "I go cruising with Mr. Onassis, because nobody else ever asked me."

Churchill had radically changed his attitude toward the sea. At twenty he had written, "I do not contemplate ever taking a sea voyage for pleasure. I shall always look upon journeys by sea as necessary evils, which have to be undergone in the carrying out of definite plans." Now, in his eighties, with time to spare and the privacy afforded by the world's most luxurious yacht, he longed for cruises and rarely ever rejected an invitation offered by his friend Onassis.

Onassis seemed to adore Churchill, catering to his every whim, treating him with the affection and respect one accords not to the aged hero, but to the aging father. That might well have been the key to their relationship. Onassis seemed to provide Churchill with the affection the statesman felt his son should have, but didn't give him; and Churchill provided Onassis with the symbol of fatherhood that he seemed

138

to be unconsciously seeking ever since the schism with his own father.

When Churchill was aboard the *Christina*, all of his commands, no matter how trivial or difficult, were carried out immediately, usually under the direct supervision of Onassis himself. Often, when the sea was particularly choppy, and just before Sir Winston retired for the evening, Onassis would take the *Christina*'s captain, Costas Anastassiadis, down to Churchill's cabin and the two men would take turns sitting or lying on his bed while talking by telephone to the bridge, attempting to find the right speed to reduce or eliminate entirely the vibrations in the room. A speed of 13 knots often seemed to cause the least amount of shaking and enable the elderly gentleman to have a peaceful night's sleep.

The two men rarely tired of each other, and Churchill admired the way Onassis could change, like himself, in midstream and go on to a new topic or endeavor. Once, when Onassis was talking about the Smyrna holocaust and reciting his reasons for the Turks having set fire to the city, Churchill suggested that they play cards instead of talk philosophy.

"Not philosophy, but history," Onassis replied.

"They are not very different," retorted Churchill, smiling. "I like living on your ship." And then the two men got down to a serious game of baccarat.

Onassis would hardly take his eyes off Churchill whenever the old man was in his "care," fetching him a glass of whiskey one moment, a blanket the next. He seemed to gain pleasure from waiting on Churchill.

Once, sitting in the Game Room, having cocktails and waiting for dinner, Churchill attempted to eat some caviar and crackers. His hand shook, and he spilled the food onto his lap. Onassis quietly pulled his chair close to Churchill's, and gently fed him teaspoonfuls of the caviar, one after the other as one might do for a baby.

Both men loved champagne, and would consume two to three bottles of Dom Perignon between them during dinner. Every evening Churchill was aboard, Onassis and all his guests would dress formally for dinner as a gesture of respect for Sir Winston, who preferred formality. When

Churchill wasn't aboard, Onassis was much more casual, usually wearing a black or white sweatshirt, a pair of nondescript gray trousers, and white deck shoes without socks.

Despite the fact that Onassis loved his friend and was aware of the debt owed by the Greeks to Churchill for delivering them from the domination of the Nazis, he was quite critical—although never to his face—of his past political history. He condemned Churchill's participation at Yalta, especially his agreement with Roosevelt to "deliver" Eastern Europe to Communist domination and his stance on decolonization.

The two men often discussed contrasts in civilization. One contemporary theme that intrigued Onassis was the economic boom of the 1950s in the United States versus the standard of living of the average French worker who, Onassis claimed, lived a better life with more leisure time—more time to spend with his family, less of a "rat race" than Americans. Once, they discussed the Sherman Adams scandal and Eisenhower's treatment of it. Churchill said: "You must either wallop a man or vindicate him." And Onassis replied callously, perhaps to indicate to Sir Winston and those within hearing that he was indeed, "ruthless": "Yes, Eisenhower just allowed him to resign. You must let your nearest and dearest go to hell when they are no longer any use to you."

Onassis and Churchill also enjoyed being by themselves, playing cards for hours and rarely talking. Churchill taught Onassis the game of bezique, a form of two-handed pinochle, and they would play for money stakes, winning or losing some $50 to $100 in the course of an evening. Often they played gin rummy or baccarat. Most of the time, Sir Winston won. On occasion, Churchill would be virtually asleep by the game's end but if he won Onassis would wake him: "Sir Winston, look, you've won!" Churchill would beam like a child.

Lord Moran, Churchill's physician and biographer, related the following conversation between Onassis and Churchill. It took place on board the *Christina*, off Martinique:

"Sir Winston, Sir Winston, I think the Prefet is a nice man. I like the Prefet. I told him that Martinique ought not to depend on sugar. They must attract American capital. They must do something. When nature provides a perfect climate and enough food, people sleep all day and do nothing. If the climate in the north of England had been less harsh and the soil more fertile, people would not have gone to sea so much. Necessity plays a big part in what men will do."

"You need not talk so loud, it must be a great effort. I can hear quite well."

"I'm sorry, Sir Winston. If people have to work very hard for sustenance, if they have to rub their hands to keep warm, they have no time for leisure. They cannot attend to the arts. Things of the spirit, things of the soul are left out of their lives. You told me, Sir Winston, your father died very young. If he had lived to your age, you might not have had to struggle so hard. Your life would have been easier, and you might not have done what you did."

"No, we were very different people."

"Yes, of course, you were different, but you would not have been driven on by necessity. My mother died when I was six. If she had lived, I might not have worked as hard as I have done."

Just as Churchill and Onassis had a strong rapport, so did their respective wives, Lady Churchill and Tina Onassis. Whenever the ship docked at a port during a cruise, the two women would go shopping and sightseeing together. While on the sea, they often spent hours talking in private, keeping what seemed a reverential distance from their two husbands. Both women were considerate and kindly toward Churchill, who could be irascible at times — although he rarely was short-tempered with Onassis.

One delicate problem that was never discussed, never even mentioned aboard ship, was Sir Winston's incontinence. His physical condition had been weakened by several strokes, and he was forced to change his clothes several times a day. His bed linens were so soiled that Onassis had to pay extra wages to the ship's laundress to have them cleaned. But the matter was always taken care of with tactful efficiency, and Onassis was vehement that Sir Winston's infirmity should not be the cause for embarrassment.

Onassis often gave Churchill gifts. At the conclusion of their Caribbean cruise in 1960, he gave Sir Winston a gold cigar box for his birthday. Engraved into the gold was a map of the islands they had visited — St. Lucia, Tobago, Puerto Rico, Antigua, Martinique, and Trinidad. In the center was etched, "Happy Birthday from Ari, November 30, 1960." It became one of Churchill's most cherished possessions.

Although Churchill made few overt gestures in thanking Onassis for his kindness, on occasion he would reciprocate. Late one afternoon, somewhere in the Aegean, there was a discussion about the Greek food that was to be served for dinner that evening. Churchill remarked that though he had been to Greece many times, he had never tasted *baklava*, the flaky, sweet pastry that is the unofficial national dessert of the country. Onassis needed to hear no more. A quiet conversation with the chef revealed that there was no *baklava* aboard, so the next morning, Onassis ordered his seaplane to fly to Athens, several hundred miles away. The pilot was directed to go to the best *baklava* bakery in the city, where he purchased a huge amount of the pastry and flew it back to the *Christina* in time for that evening's dinner.

After dinner, Churchill usually had a glass of port with a variety of cheeses. When he had completed his cheese course that night, a servant ceremoniously brought in the *baklava* and placed it in front of Sir Winston. Onassis beamed. It had cost him over $1,000 to serve his friend a slice of this pastry, but he was delighted. Churchill, realizing some of the lengths to which Onassis must have gone to obtain the dessert for him, was overwhelmed.

The next day, Churchill remained in his cabin and took all of his meals there. Late in the afternoon, he telephoned Tina and asked if she would be good enough to join him in his cabin. Although he barely had strength enough to paint anymore, he had spent the entire day doing a landscape in watercolors — for Onassis. Tina called in the ship's carpenter, a frame was constructed, and the painting was hung in the Game Room before the guests assembled for the evening's cocktails.

When Onassis entered the room, he said he smelled fresh paint, but he didn't spot the new painting at first. Nobody mentioned it; they just waited. When Onassis finally noticed it, his eyes filled with tears. The two men embraced. The painting still hangs on the wall of the Game Room, in the spot that was chosen by Sir Winston.

11

The *idea* of infidelity to Tina was exhilarating to Onassis.
Overwhelmed by the thought of his rapport with Maria
Callas, he would express those feelings with his body at
night, to Tina. She knew, immediately, that he was different, and thought that the root of his profound stirrings was
not directed toward her.

The unlikely friendship of Onassis and Churchill continued
even during the years when the Onassis name was in the society
columns almost daily as part of a scandal that rocked the jet
set.

For years, Tina and Ari had said that they would

like to entertain the famous opera singer — the only Greek ever to become renowned in grand opera — and her husband aboard the *Christina*. Onassis had met Maria in New York in the late 1930s — she was a classmate of one of his nieces — and he had followed her career, although he was not particularly fond of opera, ever since then. Earlier that year, Tina and Onassis hosted a party for Maria who sang in the Greek legend, *Medea*, at Covent Garden, the first time it had been performed in London in 80 years. Onassis was proud that a Greek, so accomplished, was being hailed as a great artist. He invited 37 guests to meet him one hour before the performance at the famous Covent Garden bar, and then presented them with complimentary tickets. The guests included a mix of British aristocracy and Greek businessmen and the newspapers ran pictures the next day of Onassis and Tina escorting Lady Churchill, one of his guests, to her seat. Callas' performance was magnificent and brought the audience cheering into the aisles. After the opera, all the guests and 170 more met at the Dorchester Hotel in a ballroom entirely decorated in pink — and pink champagne was served — to fete *La Callas*. At one point, Callas rose from her table — she was sitting with the Onassis — and spoke privately to the band leader. A moment later, the band and singer rang out "I'm Just Wild About Ari," and the guests raved.

Maria Callas was born Maria Kalogeropoulous in Brooklyn, New York, on December 3, 1923, the daughter of Greek immigrants. Her father was a druggist. Her parents returned with her to their homeland when she was a small child, and she spent the rest of her childhood and adolescence there. Although she had studied music formally from childhood and had acknowledged talent, she had difficulty gaining recognition as a serious, important singer until she reached her late twenties. She possessed a rich, powerful voice — some say one of the most dramatic in the history of opera — but she was tall, weighed 215 pounds, was myopic, appeared awkward and poorly dressed, and did not present the image of a great diva that most impressarios were eager to promote.

In 1947, she met Meneghini, a wealthy Milanese

145

industrialist, and through his important connections, made her Italian debut and first major appearance at Verona in *La Giaconda*. Meneghini managed her, arranged for serious training, encouraged her to lose weight, and generally promoted her career. Six months after meeting him, she was accepted by La Scala, the world's greatest opera house, and within a few years she was considered one of the foremost opera singers in the world, as well as one of the most fiery and temperamental. Her flourishing and impromptu exits, before, between and during acts, and her screaming arguments, with opera house managers and other singers, were notorious and brought glamour and sensationalism back into grand opera. Eventually, Meneghini gave up his own business to manage her career full-time, and in 1949 they were married. She was 26 and he was 56.

In the summer of 1959, Onassis telephoned the Meneghinis' villa in Sirmione on Lake Garda, Italy, and invited them to join himself, Tina, Sir Winston and Lady Churchill for a summer three-week cruise on the *Christina* which would end in Venice where the party would attend the annual Film Festival. Although Meneghini was not in particularly good health, he and Maria accepted the invitation, drove to Monte Carlo and set off on what they hoped would be a pleasant holiday. In addition to the three couples, the two Onassis children were aboard, as were Ari's sister Artemis and her husband, Professor Theodore Garofalides, and Gianni Agnelli of the Fiat automobile dynasty and his wife, the Princess Marella Carucciolo. Greta Garbo had also been invited but declined. It was the kind of group that both Tina and Ari enjoyed entertaining—hardly anyone, except themselves, knew anyone else and everyone was an interesting person. Tina carefully planned all the menus with the French chef and, with Onassis, organized entertainment to be held every evening.

Little Alexander became friends immediately with Agnelli, as soon as he discovered that the latter was the owner of an automobile corporation. Alexander loved cars and for the remainder of the cruise badgered Agnelli with questions about the advantages, disadvantages, speeds and other details of every type of car he could think of. Everyone, including

146

Agnelli, was amused at the 10-year-old's seriousness and persistence.

Callas had known Onassis first as her friend's uncle, then as a very rich shipping tycoon, a fellow Greek who gave lavish parties. With time to spend on board, they took an immediate interest in each other, an instant, almost electric fascination. Onassis was attracted to Callas' magnetism and intelligence and looked upon her with covetous, lollipop eyes. Now Junoesque and very lovely, she had grown into a self-assured, dynamic woman. Onassis once said to a confidant that Maria Callas exuded her sexuality when she was near him, that he could sense her lushness. To her, Onassis held great power.

She could hold her own in any conversation with anyone, including Sir Winston and Onassis, and thoroughly enjoyed exotic conversations and passionate arguments. She was entranced by his absolute confidence in himself, his great energy, and his life-style. Although the Meneghinis were com-fortable—in addition to their villa in Sirmione they owned two palaces in Verona—outside of her professional triumphs and fame which was great, they lived a quiet existence at either of their homes. Callas became caught up and exhilarated with the excitement that Onassis generated, in his desire to live well, his legendary fortune which enabled him to have anything he wanted when he so desired it, and his natural charm which caused some of the most famous of people in the world to flock around him.

From the moment she stepped aboard, Callas spoke nothing but Greek, and that almost exclusively to Onassis. This was an unusual occurrence for Onassis since he rarely spoke Greek, even to Tina, when Churchill was aboard. His conversations with Callas, therefore, took on the ambience of a secret code. By talking Greek, they felt themselves isolated from the others. They would occasionally argue about everything from the correct temperature of the wine to the state of the world economy, but genuinely enjoyed trading heated words and then lapsing from Greek, combining it with a screaming combination of Italian, English and French, seemingly all in one sentence. Meneghini, who didn't understand Greek, began to grow increasingly irritated. Oddly, neither Callas nor Onassis made any attempt to disguise their feelings for one another. They spent hours staring at each other, smiling, leaving the group to walk the decks, sometimes hand in hand. In a matter of days, everyone aboard the *Christina* could see that the two were attracted. And although a seemingly idyllic relationship was burgeoning, Maria became more and more tense as Meneghini began to observe what was happening. One evening after dinner in the main lounge when Sir Winston asked her to sing for him — and in private she would usually sing at anytime, for almost anyone — she flatly and curtly refused. "I understand," huffed Churchill, chomping down on his cigar with a philosophical air.

When the yacht docked at Portofino and then at Capri, most of the guests, with the exception of the Churchills, who preferred to remain on board — walking was painful for Sir Winston — dined at the cities' best restaurants. Always, Maria and Ari managed to sit next to each other, and they spent many evenings talking mainly to each other, toasting each other, and acting on occasion as if no one else were present.

Although Tina was used to her husband's ways, she became frustrated, depressed and angry by the openness of the association. She discussed it with Lady Churchill, who was highly sympathetic, but who could offer no helpful advice except to have patience. Perhaps Tina tried to be patient; certainly, she chose not to create a scene on the boat or when they touched shore. In public, at least, she said nothing.

Meneghini, however, could not abide the situation. Callas had become his whole world, and now he saw it slipping away from him. By the time the *Christina* docked at Istanbul, Maria and Ari felt so confident in their friendship that they went ashore alone in the early afternoon and did not return to the yacht until very late that night. The moment they left the boat, Meneghini went to pieces, screaming and raving, calling Onassis a moral leper. No one could calm him. The Churchills went quietly to their cabins and remained there for the rest of the day. Tina stolidly maintained an outward serenity as she looked after the children.

Meneghini locked himself into his stateroom and ranted all day and all night, until the couple returned. And then he refused to come out.

By the next morning, the tension aboard the *Christina* had grown unbearable. Everyone agreed that it would be best to end the cruise. Meneghini insisted that they return to Monte Carlo. At first, it was suggested that he and Maria fly to Monaco, but the gossip columnists had already become apprised of the story and were mentioning the difficulties aboard the ship—someone had spotted Ari and Maria dancing that night in Istanbul. So, it was decided to take the extra few days and sail back, to avoid any further burgeoning newspaper coverage of the cruise. When the party disembarked at Monte Carlo, they were surrounded by newspapermen and photographers, but no difficulty was even hinted at by any of the guests. Onassis implied that the cruise had been cut short simply because Churchill had wanted to return to England.

The press didn't give up, however, especially when it was learned that as soon as they returned home, both Callas and Meneghini consulted lawyers. Eventually Meneghini gave a private press conference to several Italian newspapers. He told them:

"At first, Maria sounded nebulous. She hinted that she had arrived at a turning point in her life. She acknowledged loving another man, but would not say who it was, although I urged her to be frank. Then, an hour later—to me it seemed eternity—she admitted the man she loved was Onassis. Onassis wants to glamorize his grimy tankers with the name of a great diva. They are in love like children. When we first met, Maria was a fat, clumsily dressed woman. She had no prospect of a career and I had to rent her a hotel room and put up seven hundred dollars so she could remain in Italy. I created Callas and she repaid my love by stabbing me in the back."

In her own press conference, Callas admitted that she and Meneghini had separated after ten years of marriage, but was quick to add that although the break *had* occurred during the cruise on the *Christina*, it had nothing to do with Aristotle

Onassis. "We are simply good friends," she insisted, "and he is helping me through this difficult time of my life." Callas continued to deny everything publicly, "My relations with Mr. Onassis involve business matters," she said emphatically. One possible Onassis-backed business venture, she stated, was a contract to play the lead in a film version of novelist Hans Habe's book, *Die Primadonna*.

When the press caught up with Onassis in Monte Carlo, he indicated that maybe the relationship was not Platonic, "I am a sailor and anything can happen to me." But then, perhaps thinking about how his statement would be interpreted, he added: "Sailors don't usually go for sopranos, but I would indeed be flattered to have a woman of her class fall for me."

While Onassis was toying with the press, Callas was vehemently denying her husband's charges. "These are the statements of an exasperated man who speaks under the influence of the bitterness gnawing at him. A reconciliation with my husband could not have been ruled out if the newspapers had not jumped on the story." But at the very moment Callas was blaming her woes on the media, Onassis was readying the *Christina* for a private cruise for just the two of them.

"Does this mean a separation between you and your wife?" a reporter asked Onassis. "I don't like to think about it," he responded uneasily. "We've been married for thirteen years. A father would be crazy if he wanted to separate his children from their mother."

The private cruise took Onassis and Callas on a leisurely idyll through the Mediterranean. Even the sun cooperated; the weather was warm and sunny throughout. But the press was less obliging. Wherever the boat docked, reporters and *paparazzi* hounded the couple, demanding details of their relationship. "Fairy tales," smiled Onassis, when a newsman asked if he were in love with *La Callas*. "Such news reports belong neither to this earth nor to heaven."

Onassis made additional headlines at that time because of an incident concerning another well-known and beautiful celebrity, Melina Mercouri. Onassis had known

Mercouri's father, who had been mayor of Athens, and had met Melina many times when she was a girl. One night, when Callas had flown to Rome for a performance, Onassis and Mercouri, together with actor Jules Dassin, decided to enjoy some Athenian night life. They went to the suburb of Lipessi to the Kanaki Tavern. The group drank and ate and sang, and soon, following a custom originally introduced by the Czarist officers in Imperial Russia, they began to throw plates, cups and dishes on the floor, breaking them into pieces. As the *bouzouki* music reached fever pitch, more and more plates were smashed, and Onassis and Mercouri called for more to be brought from the kitchen. By the time the evening was over, almost every plate in the restaurant was broken, newspapers chronicled the event, and Onassis paid the owners, Costas Zambetas and his wife, a check for $3,000 for the destruction.

Onassis was to meet Tina in Venice at an annual exclusive party given by Elsa Maxwell at the Hotel Royal Daneli. They had a long-standing invitation, and had promised to attend. Tina dutifully appeared and danced all night, but Onassis chose to go to Milan with Maria. The next day's papers carried the story of their nightclubbing, and a photograph of the two of them dancing. It seemed not to concern either of them that she was a full head taller than he, although many of the newspapers made cynical mention of it.

The story and photograph in the newspapers and Onassis' failure to appear in Venice were more than Tina could take. She left the *Christina*, quietly seething. By then, newspapers all over the world were carrying daily coverage of the Onassis-Callas affair. Tina flew to Paris with Alexander and Christina, met briefly with her lawyer, Sol Rosenblatt, who had flown there to confer with her, and then went on to New York.

Although there was constant speculation in the press and among her friends and family about what Tina would do, for the first two months in New York, she lived at her Sutton Square house and maintained an enigmatic silence. Onassis continued to see Callas constantly, and there were reports that simultaneous divorces between both couples — Tina and Onassis and Callas and Meneghini — were imminent.

151

Suddenly, Tina announced her intentions. At a tear-filled press conference in her home, she read a prepared statement:

"It is almost thirteen years since Mr. Onassis and I were married in New York City. Since then, he has become one of the world's richest men, but his great wealth has not brought me happiness with him, or as the world knows, has it brought him happiness with me.

"After we parted this summer in Venice, I had hoped that Mr. Onassis loved our children enough and re-spected our privacy sufficiently to meet with me — or, through lawyers, with my lawyer — to straighten out our problems. But that was not to be.

"Mr. Onassis knows positively that I want none of his wealth and that I am solely concerned with the welfare of our children. I deeply regret that Mr. Onassis leaves me no alterna-tive other than a New York suit for divorce.

"For my part, I will always wish Mr. Onassis well, and I expect that after this action is concluded he will continue to enjoy the kind of life which he apparently desires to live, but in which I have played no real part. I hope I shall be left alone with my children in peace."

Peter Hawkins, in a biography of Prince Rainier, tells the following story, which took place at that time and which indicates how Onassis was coping with the inevitable.

"The scene was London: Berkeley Square at four o'clock in the morning a handful of years ago as the nightclubs of the West End emptied their warm customers onto the city's cold streets. Most of them hailed taxis or signaled to chauffeurs waiting in the patchwork artificial lighting; the square itself was almost deserted as I drove around it on my way to a very early appoint-ment in the cause of Fleet Street. Just one man walking, slowly — one solitary figure, shoulders hunched, bent low with all the worries of the world.

"There was about this person such an absolute air of dejection, even desperation, that I drove right round the

152

square so as to return and observe him more carefully. Now he came under a street lamp and there was no mistaking the silhouette familiar from many newspaper photographs, still with the dark-tinted glasses even at four A.M. I stopped, got out of my car, and asked, 'Mr. Onassis?' The question mark was there because it seemed impossible to equate one of the world's richest men with this lonely, miserable person.

"He nodded. I asked, genuinely concerned: 'Are you all right? Is there anything I can do?'

"He replied, after hesitation, with his own question, 'Why did you stop?'

" 'You seemed so distressed. I thought perhaps you might be feeling ill. Are you sure there is nothing I can do?'

"He shook his head, gave the suggestion of a smile, and told me 'I received some news that was upsetting. I wanted a little walk on my own. It was kind of you to stop, but I just want to be alone. No doubt you will find out why, later.' "

Within a few days, everyone found out. The news was carried in every one of the world's newspapers: Tina Onassis had filed suit in New York State Supreme Court for a divorce and for the custody of Alexander and Christina.

Adultery was the only grounds for divorce in the State of New York. Maria Callas was not named in the case, the divorce brief named a "Mrs. J. R.," with whom Onassis was alleged to have had an affair. Within a short while, it was determined that "Mrs. J. R." was a well-known society figure who had lived near the Onassis when they had leased the Château de la Croë. "Mrs. J. R." denied that her relationship was anything other than friendship, but did admit that Onassis had asked her to marry him, had visited her villa a number of times, and had entertained her on the *Christina* on several cruises. Despite these facts, "Mrs. J. R." still proclaimed her innocence and threatened to sue Tina for slander. She never pressed charges.

Tina had an all-too-human reason for naming "J. R." as the correspondent in her divorce proceedings, since she could not prove adultery between Onassis and anyone else. In addition to the fact that it avoided an erroneous legal hassle,

153

it made Onassis' other relationships appear trivial and of no consequence. In effect, she was saying that no one stole her husband from her, but that the divorce was the result of an old wound of a decade past that had caused the schism.

There were many attempts to get the Onassis' to reconcile. Princess Grace flew from Monaco to New York to talk with Tina. At first she appeared encouraged, but ultimately she could not get her friend to withdraw her divorce petition. Lady Churchill wrote, called, and sent encouragement. She suggested that Ari and Tina consider a rapprochment. Tina's mother and father tried appealing to both Ari and Tina to at least consider a temporary reconciliation. Livanos flew to the *Christina* and tried to persuade Onassis to "come to his senses." Livanos was adamant that his daughter should not go through an adultery case in order to receive the divorce, and contended that since money was not an object (Livanos was one of the world's richest men; gifts and trusts he had given his daughter, and gifts she had received from Onassis during their marriage, had made Tina many times a millionaire in her own right; she had neither the need nor inclination to ask for alimony), the resulting highly-publicized divorce action would not only hurt her and the children, but would hurt the entire Greek shipping fraternity.

Onassis and Tina met briefly in Paris, and he begged her not to go through with the divorce, or certainly not to do it in New York, although it was clear to both of them that a reconciliation was out of the question. Shortly after that, Tina broke her right leg while skiing in Switzerland. She was transferred to a hospital in England and Ari visited her once again to try to talk her out of the divorce. She was adamant about going through with it, but had begun to change her mind about filing in New York. Lady Churchill also visited her, attempting to cheer her up, and on her second visit, was accompanied by one of Sir Winston's relatives, the Marquess of Blandford, a tall, handsome young man known as "Sonny." Soon, Sonny was visiting Tina on his own. When she was released, she was his guest at Blenheim Palace, the home of his father, the Duke of Marlborough.

Instead of going through with the New York divorce,

In 1968, Jacqueline Kennedy at 39, the widow of the slain U.S. President John F. Kennedy, shocked the world when she married Aristotle Onassis, a man old enough to be her father at 62, in addition to being a foreigner and a non-Catholic. The marriage was the high point in Onassis' life. Here the couple celebrate after the ceremony at a champagne reception aboard the *Christina*.

In the fall of 1971, Jackie and Ari spent time vacationing in the Mediterranean and docked the *Christina* at the isle of Capri. Their window-shopping of the city's main jewelry section caused huge crowds to gather.

(Sipa-Press)

In celebrating her fortieth birthday, Ari took Jackie to a seaside nightclub outside Athens where they danced and sang until past dawn.
(Globe Photos)

Onassis was very close to his stepson, John Kennedy, Jr. Here, shortly before Onassis' death, they enter his limousine to return to Paris after a ride in the French countryside. Jackie can be seen in the background.   *(Sipa-Press)*

Onassis adored his only son, Alexander, whom he was grooming to eventually take over his vast holdings and business interests. Here, in 1967, they confer aboard the *Christina*.
(Sipa-Press)

After the death of Alexander, at the age of 25 in an airplane crash in Greece, Onassis never recovered emotionally. Grief-stricken, he nevertheless immediately began to teach Christina, shown with him at Alexander's funeral, the intricacies and secrets of his financial operations. *(Sipa-Press)*

Onassis had great affection for his daughter, Christina. Here they are on Onassis' yacht, which he named after her. *(Globe Photos)*

Onassis was very friendly with Anwar Sadat, whom he greets in Cairo at the wedding of Sadat's daughter. Onassis was accompanied by Christina and his sister Artemis.
(Sipa-Press)

During his lifetime — whether he was married or single — Onassis wined and dined, and often courted, many of the world's most beautiful women. Shortly before his death, he spent an evening with actress Marisa Berenson touring the nightclubs of Paris.   *(Sipa-Press)*

Although having trouble with his eyes as a result of myasthenia gravis, Onassis dined out alone at Maxim's in Paris early in 1975 when Jackie was in New York. This is one of the last pictures taken of him before the illness became totally debilitating.

(Sipa-Press)

Seen through the window at the American hospital in Paris, Jackie and
Christina Onassis talk with the doctor and stand vigil at Onassis' bedside.
(Sipa-Press)

Jacqueline Kennedy Onassis, a widow for the second time, attends the funeral of
her husband, Aristotle Onassis, who died in Paris in March 1975. With her is
Onassis' sister Artemis. *(Sipa-Press)*

Tina eventually went to court in Alabama and claimed mental cruelty. She received a satisfactory judgment, was given custody of the two children, made a settlement for the children's support. Within a year, Tina remarried and became the Marchioness of Blandford. That marriage was a relatively short one and ended in divorce, also. Tina eventually married Niarchos, after the death, by an overdose of drugs, of her sister Eugenie. Friends of Tina claim that she had always been in love with Niarchos and had hoped that he would have "selected" her to have married, instead of her sister, in the 1940s. Tina's reaction, they have opined, was to marry Onassis.

Naturally, Onassis at first became outraged and embittered when he heard that Tina, his former wife but still someone he felt deeply about, was going to marry his arch-enemy and rival. Even their two children seemed disillusioned with their mother for marrying someone whom they were raised to distrust. This distrust had heightened when their Aunt Eugenie died under circumstances which precipitated a long and tense trial.

Eventually, Onassis calmed down but not before snubbing Tina at the funeral of his friend Winston Churchill. Arrangements had been carefully made that Tina and Onassis did not sit anywhere near each other during the service.

Onassis' relationships, even those which endured for twenty or more years, were quite fragile because of his often unpredictable and explosive behavior and because many of those around him always expected financial favors of one sort or another from him.

Pahaghis Vergottis, a Greek shipowner who was a neighbor of Onassis on the Riviera, was a close friend for over thirty years. The friendship ended heatedly and dramatically in a London court trial in April 1967. Maria Callas played the role of Delilah in this rather bizarre opera of friendship and jealousy.

Vergottis, sixteen years older than Onassis, was introduced to Callas at one of Ari's very chic dinner parties in London's Dorchester Hotel in June 1959. "He is one of my dearest friends, if not the best I have," Onassis told her. In a short period of time, the diva and Vergottis also became close friends. Maria loved him like a father, and he worshipped her every move. Onassis, Vergottis, and Callas became an inseparable threesome.

Vergottis was always advising Callas on her financial affairs, and continually prompted her to invest her money wisely to provide for the future. Onassis and Vergottis agreed that Callas should have a ship of her own. They believed it would be a sound financial move on her part, and perhaps provide some enjoyment for the three of them as they watched it bring in profits.

Vergottis found a 27,000-ton tanker which was being built in Spain. The ship, later christened the *Artemesion II*, was for sale for about $3 million. The trio formed a Liberian corporation.

One evening during a lengthy telephone conversation, they argued about her plans to make a German film of *Tosca*. Vergottis felt it would help her career, but she and Onassis felt it might hurt her reputation. Maria tore into him and they argued loudly and violently. Later, Maria apologized but somehow Vergottis got it into his head and was certain that Onassis and Maria had plotted against him. He was jealous that she was taking Onassis' advice and not his. Vergottis was deeply hurt from Maria's blast and wanted to strike back. Arbitrarily, he refused to give up Maria's 25 shares in the company and announced that her down payment was merely a loan from the Overseas Bulk Carriers.

In order to protect Callas' interests, Onassis and Maria had to file an action against Vergottis to reclaim the 25 shares of stock. This was just what Vergottis wanted. He used the trial as a soapbox to discuss the personal aspects of the Onassis-Callas relationship. During the trial, Vergottis stated that Onassis often mistreated Callas, that Onassis hated his brother-in-law Niarchos and that Ari was "black in his heart." Much of the questioning at the trial centered around their relationship.

The court decided in Callas' favor. In the judge's decision, Vergottis was cited as a troublemaker. "Vergottis'

156

mind is a tortuous one," he stated. "I formed a wholly favorable view of Mr. Onassis and Madame Callas, but take an unfavorable view of Mr. Vergottis." Even though Onassis was debased by Vergottis, he felt he must condemn the judge's statement as "the humiliation of an old friend." Vergottis asked for and was granted a new trial, and once again the court found in the favor of Onassis and Callas.

"This naked rock is bathed in a naked light—a light unlike any other light on the surface of the earth. It is a light that can be drunk and tasted, full of ripeness; light that filters through flesh and marble; light that is almost palpable. It fumes and glares, and seems to have a life of its own. It is in perpetual movement, flashing off the sea onto the rocks, flashing from one mountain to another and back again, spilling over the valleys."

Jackie completed reading the paragraph from Robert Payne's *The Splendour of Greece*, stood up from the chaise on the terrace and looked out to the deep turquoise of the Ionian. That strange, crisp, clear, shining light was present, and she was filled with the majesty of it. She felt serene, romantic, captured by all that Greece was and is.

She went inside to where Onassis was sleeping on the white canvas sofa in front of the fireplace, his shoes and shirt off, wearing only his rumpled gray trousers. She was dressed in white silk harem pants and a matching blouse that looked something like a *dashiki*. She wore Turkish slippers and had the walk, not of a model, but of an athlete; her years of riding and skiing gave her a pronounced swagger.

As she stood, staring at him, he awoke. "Jacqueline!" he mumbled, sliding himself up to a sitting position. "I was asleep." She smiled and said, "I know," and walked to the grand piano at the other side of the room. They had been married two days previously. He had never heard her play, although she had insisted that the villa on Skorpios be equipped with a piano. Now she chose one of Chopin's "Etudes"; Onassis watched and listened to her silently, peering over the back of the sofa. When she was finished, he applauded enthusiastically. "Brava!"

"Teles, let's not go down to *Christina* tonight. Let's stay up here. I can't face the crew. I want to be alone, with you," she said softly.

Onassis smiled. He stood, now fully awake, and went out into the approaching twilight and climbed into his jeep, parked on a special road that led right up to the side of the house. She stood beside the car as he started the motor.

"I'll order dinner and let them bring it up here," he said.

"Why don't you send one of the servants?" she asked.

"I want to shave."

"But there's a razor here."

"I know, but I *like* to shave on the ship."

He was gone. In a little over an hour, he returned, showered and shaved, now dressed in a black turtleneck sweater and black pants. Jackie had also changed into black slacks and a red turtleneck, had lit the candles on the dining room table and made a pitcher of vodka martinis. The remaining light from the last minutes of dusk set the room aglow with copper. "I want ouzo tonight," he said, and poured himself an impossibly large glass of the milky-white liqueur.

Soon, two servants, wearing white jackets over black tee shirts with the word CHRISTINA emblazoned across their chests, arrived with a vehicle filled with food. Jackie went into one of the bedrooms to wait for them to leave. Onassis supervised the placement of the food. Each dish was served in a silver bowl or platter and the men ceremoniously, but without speaking, arranged them on the table, removed the covers, and were gone in minutes.

All Jackie could do was laugh when she came out and saw the table before her. Onassis smiled mischievously.

There was enough food for at least a dozen people. Onassis explained some of the delicacies with which Jackie was unfamiliar. There were tiny birds from Cyprus, called *beccafica*, preserved for over a year in vinegar, to be eaten delicately, with the fingers, in their entirety, including the bones; a large pheasant under glass; platters of broiled lamb; six different types of vegetables; slices of yellow onions; baskets of freshly baked breads and rolls; dishes of huge fresh figs, iced grapes, plump black olives, chestnuts and almonds; feta and five other types of white and yellow cheeses; an entire watermelon; oranges, bee's jelly, *baklava*, halvah, and a many-tiered tray of French pastries.

Onassis opened a bottle of Dom Perignon and filled two glasses. Jackie stayed with her martini. Onassis himself finally finished the bottle of champagne.

After dinner, Onassis carefully constructed a fire in the fireplace. They sat alone, watching it, saying nothing. The room darkened completely except for the light of the fire and the two candles, in hurricane lamps, atop the table.

Although Onassis first met Jacqueline Kennedy at a dinner party in Georgetown in the 1950s when John F. Kennedy was still a senator, they hardly exchanged more than a few words. A year later when Jack and Jackie made a trip to the south of France to visit Jack's parents, Rose and Joseph Kennedy, they were invited aboard the *Christina*, docked at Monte Carlo, to meet Sir Winston Churchill who was about to begin that much heralded and aborted cruise with Onassis and Maria Callas and her husband. The young senator and his wife were enchanted to be given the opportunity to visit Churchill aboard the world's most opulent yacht. They arrived in the late afternoon for cocktails. Churchill and Kennedy immediately flung themselves into a politically nostalgic conversation that revolved around some of the stories that J.F.K.'s father had told him about his experiences as U. S. Ambassador to the Court of St. James's from 1937 to 1941. Kennedy as a history major at Harvard, regarded Churchill with great admiration and thought of him as one of his heroes. Churchill was not unaware of John F. Kennedy; he remarked how interesting he found the young man's thesis, *Why England Slept*, which was eventually published in London.

Years later, in 1963, during Churchill's last visit to the United States, he talked again with John F. Kennedy and also aboard the *Christina*. The yacht was docked in New York's 79th Street boat basin in the Hudson River, and Kennedy telephoned Churchill, asking him to pay a visit to the White House. With failing health, Churchill declined but promised to come "at some later time."

While the two men talked, Onassis gave Jackie a personal tour of the yacht; even though Maria Callas and her husband were already aboard, somehow the two women never met. Jackie was enormously impressed with the *Christina* and for years afterward continually made references to it in conversations with her friends. If she were equally impressed with Onassis, there were no outward signs. "Mr. Onassis, I have fallen in love with your ship," she said. As for Onassis, although he was respectful, there was nothing more than the politeness of a dutiful host shown toward Jackie. He already had his mind and heart focused on Maria Callas.

Almost ten years later, now as the wife of the President of the United States and fast becoming one of the most famous world celebrities in her own right, Jackie, on an official state visit to England with J.F.K., briefly visited her sister, Princess Lee Radziwill and her husband, Prince Stanislas. As Kennedy flew home to Washington, Jackie and the Radziwills made an impromptu visit to Greece at the invitation of Premier Constantine Karamanlis. It was Jackie's first trip there. They were met at the Athens airport by the Premier and his wife, who escorted them by motorcade to Kavouri on the outskirts of Athens to the palatial villa of Greek shipowner Markos Nomikos and his wife Aspasia.

Onassis had met Lee Radziwill for the first time in London, just shortly before Jackie had arrived for her visit. They had been introduced at a post-Ascot formal garden party at the home of a mutual friend and took an immediate liking to each other. Gossip columnists were soon tracking the couple as they wined and dined alone in some of London's finest restaurants.
     When the two sisters arrived in Greece, Onassis was invited by Nomikos to a cocktail party in their honor. He paid his respects to Jackie, but spent most of his time talking to Lee, a situation that might indicate, at least at that time, that no romantic inclinations toward Jackie had begun to affect Onassis, at least not publicly. Doris Lilly, in her book *Those Fabulous Greeks*, stated that "Twice in his life Aristotle Onassis had been linked with two sisters and twice he had married the one no one was watching." Jackie and her party spent weeks cruising the Aegean on Nomikos' yacht and she fell helplessly in love with the romance and grandeur of Greece, vowing to come back "again and again."
     In the early part of the summer of 1963, Onassis and Lee cruised on the Aegean aboard the *Christina*. Later that summer, Jackie's infant son, Patrick, died forty hours after being born, and both she and Jack Kennedy were desperately depressed over the tragedy. Jackie wanted to see Lee, her closest friend, and called her. Lee was dining with Onassis in Athens at that very moment and Onassis immediately offered Jackie the private use of the *Christina* for a cruise to help speed her recovery and perhaps renew her perspective. Lee encouraged Jackie to accept the invitation and promised to accompany her on the trip. Jackie accepted. Onassis also offered to stay in Athens while the two sisters were aboard—in order to

avoid any scandal — but Jackie insisted that he go along. As a compromise, Onassis said he would stay below deck or in his private cabin whenever they were in port and that it would be announced to the press that he was not a part of the cruise.

Franklin D. Roosevelt, Jr., and his wife, Susan, accompanied Jackie — along with a Secret Service agent — to Europe and were her official escorts during the cruise. In addition, Onassis' sister Artemis was aboard, as was Lee's husband, Prince Stanislas. Before they got underway, Onassis announced, "The ship will go wherever Mrs. Kennedy wants it to go. She is the captain."

In preparation for the voyage, Onassis attempted to anticipate Jackie's possible wants. The *Christina* was stocked with an abundance of rare vintage wines, eight varieties of caviar, fruits, meats and fish, flown from all over the world. So that she would feel comfortable about her appearance, Onassis had two hairdressers and a Swedish masseur come aboard for the cruise. There was also a small orchestra for dancing in the evenings. Not counting the food, drink and salaries of the crew, just these amenities cost over $40,000.

The first stop was the island of Lesbos, where Jackie and Lee and a few of the other passengers toured the island. As agreed, Onassis was nowhere to be found as the local photographers took pictures of the famous party. At Crete, Jackie and the other guests visited the ruins of the Palace of Knossos, again without Onassis, and photographs of Jackie taken at that time show a progressive day-by-day recuperation. After a week aboard the *Christina*, Jackie seemed radiant and relaxed.

The *Christina* then sailed to Turkey and docked at Smyrna, the birthplace of Onassis. Everyone, including Jackie and Roosevelt, insisted that Onassis go ashore, and he agreed. He acted as the tour guide for the city, showing the group where he had lived, where his father's factory had stood, the streets he walked going to school. Within a matter of hours, his photograph stepping off the gangplank of the *Christina* and strolling the streets of his hometown was flashed across the globe. A few days later, when the ship docked at Istanbul, there were even more photographers and newsmen to greet Onassis and his guests. Callas was reported to have said: "He is obsessed with famous women. He was obsessed with me because I was famous. Now she and her sister, they have obsessed him and they are even more famous." Jackie also had begun to receive criticism in Washington for her association with a man who had been convicted of a crime by the U. S. Justice Department. A Republican Congressman, Oliver Bolton of Ohio, castigated Jackie on the floor of the House, questioning the propriety of the wife of the U. S. President. He indicated that she and Roosevelt were guests of a foreigner who had been at odds with the U. S. government, who was "turning over to the disposal of a Presidential and Department of Commerce [Roosevelt] party a luxury ship, with a sixty-man crew including two coiffeurs and dance bands, at a personal cost of many tens of thousands of dollars." Roosevelt was Under Secretary of Commerce at that time and Bolton also pointed out that Onassis was attempting to benefit from Roosevelt's relationship with and influence over the U. S. Maritime Administration.

Kennedy, although at first enthusiastic about his wife's trip, began to seriously worry whether the adverse criticism Jackie was receiving would affect his campaign for the next election. He telephoned the *Christina* on a number of occasions and attempted to persuade Jackie to return to Washington. Jackie, however, was having a marvelous time and was not going to allow criticism from a mere U. S. Congressman — nor the demands of her fun-loving husband — to restrict her life.

The U. S. Congress and the American public could not know, of course, that what was really happening on the cruise was that Aristotle Onassis was falling in love with the First Lady of the United States. At first they were quite formal toward each other, not sincerely though, waiting for the other to make a gesture of closeness. Neither could acknowledge the growing affinity they felt. Slowly, mainly through Onassis' natural charm and instinctive ability to "handle" awkward situations, they began to relax. They got along famously, speaking voraciously in English, Spanish and French. Jackie was soon fascinated by Onassis' energy, his charisma in a ruthless pursuit of her, his earthiness, his intelligent attention to detail and most of all, his ostentatious romancing. At each port, he lavished gifts on her—everything from a golden bracelet to a straw hat. He all at once offered to be her friend, provider, companion, father, confessor and possible lover. He found her to be strikingly, sadly beautiful, fragile but insurgent, attractively inscrutable, never quite revealing what she felt emotionally but intensely interested in his conversation. And even her imperiousness was attractive to him: she acted as a queen and demanded complete control over her own environment. Onassis, with his own airline and his own fleet, his houses all over the world, was sovereign of his own personal kingdom and was eager to give her the privacy she demanded.

They talked of their families, their backgrounds. She was amused and fascinated at his seemingly unending supply of anecdotes, and she was impressed that even on their cruise he was able to constantly conduct and control his businesses throughout the world. Cables and telephone calls from heads of state and the presidents of the world's largest corporations arrived demandingly and Onassis, sometimes even between dinner courses, dictated replies and returned calls that had multi-million dollar implications. Whereas Jack Kennedy ruled a country, Onassis seemed to rule the world. The *Christina* was busier than the Oval Office.

Most evenings, during good weather, after a midnight supper had been served on deck, the couple sat alone and talked, sometimes until dawn. She was thoroughly aware of Onassis' growing attraction to her. Even though the risk of scandal was enormous, Onassis constantly pursued her on that cruise.

Journalist Peter Evans reported that in the autumn of 1967 at a small cocktail party at the George V Hotel in Paris, Onassis made this perceptive statement about Jacqueline Kennedy:

"She's a totally misunderstood woman. Perhaps she even misunderstands herself. She's being held up as a model of propriety, constancy, and so many of those boring American female virtues. She's now utterly devoid of mystery. She needs a small scandal to bring her alive. A peccadillo, an indiscretion.

Something should happen to her to win our fresh compassion. The world loves to pity fallen grandeur."

When the cruise ended, Onassis presented Lee with a string of pearls and Jackie a mammoth diamond and ruby necklace. Jackie flew from Athens to Rabat, where briefly she was the guest of Morocco's King Hassan II, and then returned to Washington, two months after she had left. She was tanned, rested, effervescent, and refreshed by the Mediterranean breezes and the flush of a new and exciting companion. The cruise had been exactly what she needed. One of the first things she did when she returned to the White House was to make sure that all of Onassis' addresses — Paris, Glyfada, Monte Carlo — were entered by her secretary in Jackie's personal address book. She then ordered a large silver cigarette box from Tiffany's and had it sent to Onassis, together with a note thanking him for his hospitality on the trip. She talked to everyone about Onassis as an "alive and vital person" and thought his invitation to her was "an act of kindness."

Benjamin Bradlee, in his book *Conversations with Kennedy*, stated that Kennedy told Jackie that he believed that her trip was damaging to him politically and that she should make it clear to Onassis that he should not come to the United States until the election of 1964 was over. Bradlee went on to say that Kennedy "noted that what he called 'Jackie's guilt feelings' might work to his advantage.

" 'Maybe now you'll come with us to Texas next month,' he said with a smile.

"And Jackie answered, 'Sure I will, Jack.' "

Shortly after that, when discussing with Jackie who Kennedy's successor might be in 1968 (since he was confident he would win in 1964) and ruling out Lyndon B. Johnson, his then Vice President, she said, "Well, who then?" Kennedy replied: "It was going to be Franklin (Roosevelt), but you and Onassis fixed that."

Onassis was in Hamburg on November 22, 1963, overseeing the last construction details before the launching of a new tanker, the *Olympic Chivalry*. While waiting to sit down to

166

dinner an aide told him of the news of the assassination of John F. Kennedy. He was deeply shocked and called Lee immediately. She insisted that Onassis accompany her and her husband to the funeral, and within a few hours Onassis received a phone call from Angier Biddle Duke, Chief of Protocol, inviting him to be a house guest—one of the few outside the family—at the White House during the funeral proceedings. William Manchester stated in *Death of a President*:

"Rose Kennedy dined upstairs with Stash Radziwill; Jacqueline Kennedy, her sister, and Robert Kennedy were served in the sitting room. The rest of the Kennedys ate in the family dining room with their house guests, McNamara, Phyllis Dillon, David Powers and Aristotle Socrates Onassis, the shipowner who provided comic relief, of sorts. They badgered him mercilessly about his yacht and his Man of Mystery aura. During coffee, the Attorney General (Bobby) came down and drew up a formal document stipulating that Onassis give half his wealth to help the poor in Latin America. It was preposterous (and obviously unenforceable), and the Greek millionaire signed it in Greek."

From the time that Onassis paid his condolences to Jacqueline Kennedy in 1963 until 1968, he saw her frequently and usually in private. He was in his own words, "the invisible man." When Jackie moved into her fifteen-room duplex apartment at 1040 Fifth Avenue, overlooking New York's Central Park, Onassis, who owned a permanent suite at the Hotel Pierre, just a short distance away, would often secretly visit her. Perhaps the idea of what seemed to be a ludicrous match to many—that of the short, squat, flamboyant Oriental and the tall, regal, beautifully elegant widow and fairy princess, some thought of her as America's first queen since the wife of George III—was what prevented the usually relentless press from discovering the liaison.

Jackie spent long weekends at Onassis' apartment in Paris; they occasionally dined out in less than famous New York restaurants; Onassis was Jackie's guest at several dinner parties at her Fifth Avenue apartment.

During this time, Jackie was also escorted to a variety of functions, parties and cultural events by a number of both eligible and ineligible celebrities, including Leonard Bernstein, Mike Nichols, Randolph Churchill, George Plimpton, Frank Sinatra, John Kenneth Galbraith, Arthur Schlesinger, Jr., and Lord Harlech, all of whom served as a screen, knowingly or not, to her incongruous romance with Onassis. As Jackie's involvement with those minor planets progressed ever so slowly, Onassis was still seen constantly and openly with Maria Callas, dining at Maxim's, cruising on the *Christina*, attending parties and balls on three continents.

When the aircraft carrier *John F. Kennedy* was commissioned, Ari was invited to attend the ceremonies at Newport News, Virginia. Jackie, however, was unaware that he was on the guest list. After the speeches were made and Jackie was talking in the center of a group of well-wishers, Ari casually approached her. When she spotted him out of the corner of her eye, she stopped her monologue in mid-sentence, spun around and beamed: "Oh, Ari, I didn't know you were here!" Some of Jackie's friends who were present at that time mark her exuberance at seeing Onassis as the first open, unguarded signal of her interest in him.

In the spring of 1968, Jackie and Ari began appearing in public. They dined at a Greek restaurant in New York called Mykonos and their guests were Margot Fonteyn, Rudolph Nureyev and Onassis' daughter, Christina. At a small party Jackie gave at another charming restaurant, Sign of the Dove, Onassis appeared late, but left with her about 2 A.M., at the party's end.

At an intimate dinner party given at the home of one of Jackie's friends, Onassis invited Garbo, specifically so the two women could meet. Garbo had expressed affection for both Jackie and J.F.K. and was particularly charming and friendly when she finally met Jackie. They talked and laughed, but quite early in the evening, living up to her reputation of wanting to be alone, Garbo rose and said, "I must go. I am getting intoxicated." She said her good-byes and quietly left alone.

That summer, Jackie and Ari traveled together to such diverse cities as Palm Beach, Florida, Newport, Rhode

Island, and Southhampton, New York, and she took several short cruises aboard the *Christina*, to St. Thomas and Nassau, in the Caribbean.

The evening before she was due on board the *Christina* for one cruise, in May 1968, Onassis ordered a number of framed photographs of Jackie and J.F.K. to be hung at various places in the salon and other rooms, more as a token of interest and respect than for any other reason. Her personal maid had arrived aboard before she did and when she spotted the photographs she quickly informed Onassis' secretary that except in the children's rooms, there were no pictures of John F. Kennedy in the New York apartment. Jackie found it too painful. Within a matter of minutes, the photos were taken off the walls and put into storage, and Jackie never knew about it.

Onassis was constantly with Jackie and it was noted that they always took tea together, alone, in the late afternoon. It was during one of those private moments, somewhere in the Caribbean, that Onassis proposed marriage to Jackie and they discussed the possibility for days. Ari's proposal did not come as a surprise to Jackie, nor was it an act of impetuosity on his part. He had discussed it at length with his sister Artemis, who had given her token approval. Then he spoke to Lee to gauge what Jackie's reaction might be. Lee, who was highly in favor of the match, called Jackie and told her that Onassis was considering a proposal. What Jackie's initial reaction to that information relayed by Lee was not known. When Onassis phoned Jackie, however, to invite her on the Caribbean cruise and mentioned that he had something to discuss with her, she readily accepted the invitation, knowing the proposal was imminent.

Onassis realized that if he married Jacqueline Kennedy, he would be criticized for adding another bauble to his already resplendent life. He was one of the richest men in the world, capable of collecting almost anything he desired, and he was known for his compulsive acquisitions of houses, ships, corporations, works of art and even people. He was outrageously attracted to Jackie—indeed, deeply in love with her—but also had doubted whether a marriage would be wise;

169

nevertheless, he continued to push for it. To Onassis, the pursuit was equally as exciting and absorbing as the prize.

Jackie, who through her tragic widowhood had been enshrined as a popular American saint, felt somewhat more hesitant and skeptical than Onassis. If she married a non-Catholic, a well-known philanderer and divorced man, she stood an excellent chance of being excommunicated from the Church. There was also the problem of her children, Caroline and John, who were 11 and 8 at that time. During the few times they met, Caroline was at best, sullen and reserved toward Onassis and on some occasions overtly hostile. John was more open and friendly toward Onassis, but the question of whether he could ever consider this 62-year-old man his father was one that disturbed Jackie. Each time Onassis met the children, he brought gifts and toys for them, but the role he seemed to be developing with them was less paternal than that of a rich uncle or kindly grandfather.

Jackie was also very much a part of the Kennedy clan and, for the children's benefit, if not for her own, wanted to continue that relationship. Her marriage to Onassis might possibly sever all ties with the Kennedys who at that time considered Onassis a sensation-seeking vulgarian with a questionable background and dubious motivation for wanting to get close to Jackie, whom they felt genuinely protective toward.

Bobby Kennedy, who was vigorously campaigning for the Presidency, held a powerful influence over Jackie ("I'd go to hell for him," she once said), and before giving Onassis her answer, she telephoned Bobby from the *Christina*, telling him that she was considering marriage. Bobby, it has been reported, did not at first take her seriously, but as a safeguard to the nostalgic and heartstrung votes he would have received for the nomination and possible election by her support that year, asked her to wait until the election was over. She agreed. Later, when he came to realize that she was serious, he strenuously objected to the match and dispatched Ethel and Joan to New York to see if they could talk Jackie out of it. They couldn't.

Despite the obvious obstacles that might prevent the marriage of Jackie and Ari, the chemistry between them was, they felt, a perfect amalgam of opposites, combined with some very real and practical reasons to wed.

Onassis offered Jackie security, unlimited wealth, privacy, mobility, warmth and freedom. He made it clear to her that if they married, she would be free to go wherever and whenever she pleased — with him or without him — and that she would enjoy the position of being among the richest women in the world. There was a certain randy charm about Onassis, an earthiness and extravagance that she found fascinating. Onassis was a born orator and Jackie would sit and listen to him spin off tales and stories — often racy — by the hour. Occasionally she would comment gently, in her whispering, almost inaudible way. She was never bored with him. He could keep a dinner party of some of the world's most sophisticated conversationalists spellbound as he told about his privileged childhood in Turkey, his whaling days in Antarctica, his relationships with Callas, Churchill, Eva Peron, Greta Garbo, speaking variously any one — or a combination — of seven languages, according to the delight and abilities of his audience. He talked with color, wit, imagination and sensitivity, but he was also capable of breaking wind uninhibitedly in public — with great beef and sonance — and then laughing uproariously and with relish. Even Jackie, as everyone else, could not help but drop her reserve and laugh with him. She simply never knew anyone quite as free or exotic as Aristotle Onassis, a paradoxical blend of raconteur and ruffian. He was so different from John F. Kennedy, who rarely even kissed her in public, let alone said or did anything that was spontaneous and uncalculated. Her friends also, were all intellectuals, proper, cultured men of the salon who rarely exposed their inner feelings. Onassis was a man of the pier but with the cocksureness of a king. At first, Jackie would almost swoon with the delight of being his.

The question of whether Onassis could "replace" J.F.K. in Jackie's heart was not as muddied as one might think. Although the marriage was not thoroughly devoid of affectionate and tender moments, and she was, of course, interested in keeping J.F.K.'s memory alive, she had long since become disillusioned by his reputation as the most aggressive woman chaser

171

in contemporary American politics. Onassis was also very much aware of Kennedy's womanizing and once remarked, after J.F.K.'s death: "Jack was a very naughty boy."

Although her children didn't seem to be fond of Onassis, Jackie began to feel that would change. He genuinely liked Caroline and John and was greatly concerned over their welfare, both financially and emotionally. If Jackie thought she was too "good" to marry a Greek god, as someone cynically remarked, it was obvious that she now felt at least one Greek man was worthy of her, and Onassis was the one.

To Onassis, having Jackie as his wife became his all-consuming goal. She would be the ultimate accomplishment of his life, much greater in his own personal scale of values than being the richest man on earth. "I am always searching for the consummate woman," he once said, perhaps too flippantly, but if he were sincere, there is reason to believe he had found her.

Despite the obvious impediments, inwardly he was astounded that she did not immediately accept his offer of marriage, and yet her hesitance initiated an even deeper desire on his part. There was little in this world that Onassis failed to acquire and with all speed, when he was determined to do so. Jackie's temporary reluctance, perhaps an instinctive feminine maneuver to secure what she really wanted, tempered his resolve even deeper. He became obsessed with the idea of marrying her.

By the time she left the *Christina* to fly back to New York, Jackie had agreed in *principle* to marry Onassis, but without giving him a formal acceptance, one that could be made public or an agreement from which plans could be made.

Only a few weeks later, on June 5, 1968, Bobby Kennedy was assassinated in Los Angeles. Onassis' first reaction was somewhat selfish and cruel. He said to a friend, "It's a tragedy for America, but for Jackie . . . she's finally free of the Kennedys."

But was she? After the initial shock began to fade, Onassis discerned a grimmer implication: Jackie, having to relive an almost exact copy of her previous tragedy, might be unable to respond to him. Wracked with this new depression,

Jackie's feelings of love could easily be darkened, if not forever, at least for a much longer time than Onassis felt he could wait. As it developed, Jackie experienced a quite different emotion. Frischauer, in his biography of Jackie, describes her feelings and ultimate reactions:

" . . . Bobby's death filled her cup to the brim leaving no more room for suffering; . . . anger was replacing sorrow and turning her against the violent society which she held responsible for her own bereavement. If America ever had a claim on her after Jack's death, that claim was now forfeited. If she ever had any doubt or obligation to consider the impact of her action on the political prospects of the Kennedys, they were resolved by the shots that ended Bobby's life. For her, escape was the only way out. Jackie was shedding the Kennedy shackles . . . her decision to marry Onassis was made at the grave of Robert F. Kennedy."

If Jackie's resolution was not made in its entirety at that time, it is clear that her feelings of ambivalence toward Onassis were instantly resolved. He flew to Los Angeles and served as a protector toward her then, as well as at the funeral back in New York City at St. Patrick's Cathedral. She was in a state of panic and disbelief, occasionally lapsing into dialogue that indicated that she was confusing both assassinations, at one point even temporarily believing that she was still First Lady.

In August, Onassis insisted that Jackie fly to Skorpios for a recuperative vacation. The couple stayed aboard the *Christina*, anchored at the island's private dock, and spent most of their days alone at a small beach house in a remote part of the island. In the evenings, there were parties aboard ship: Onassis' sister Artemis was a guest, as were Alexander and Christina and a number of Greek shipping tycoons and friends, there to make money and talk business.

Once again, Jackie began to relax and forget. The sea, the sun, the air of Greece worked wonders on her, and whenever she began to slip into a depressive state, there was Onassis, clowning, bellowing, charming everyone, including her.

Onassis had a *bouzouki* band brought from Athens,

and an enterprising journalist, Nikos Mastorakis, sneaked aboard as the group's manager. In a story in *Life*, he stated:

"Two pretty girls, one blonde and the other dark and with her leg in a cast, are there. All, including Jackie and Telis (her pet name for Ari), seemed pleased with their lives and they ate black caviar and red tomatoes. Jackie, who is resplendent in a red blouse and long gypsy skirt, prefers the vodka. She leans close when Telis whispers in her ear. At dinner Onassis eats his lamb like a youth. She eats little and nibbles white grapes. But at 4 A.M., with Mr. Moon above, the sweet Mrs. Kennedy sings with Telis when he starts *Adios Muchachos* and I feel they are close."

Eventually, all the guests departed and perhaps for the first time in the life of the *Christina*, Onassis had both the telephones and ship's radio disconnected. The only way to reach either Jackie or him was by telegram brought by boat from the larger island of Lefkas, nearby.

Just before Onassis cut off all communications with the outside world, he had received a transatlantic call from Ted Kennedy, asking if he might come to Skorpios "to talk things over." Onassis instantly agreed and the Senator flew immediately to Greece.

According to Gail Cameron's biography of Rose Kennedy, *Rose*, Ted went to Hyannisport to solicit his mother's blessing before he went on the trip. "Mother," he said "I'm going to take a cruise on Onassis' yacht." Rose looked at him and asked: "Well, what's so extraordinary about that?" Kennedy broke the news: "Onassis is very much in love with Jackie." There was a short silence. Finally, Rose said: "I've known Onassis for fifteen years. He's a fine man."

Later, Jackie brought Onassis to Rose Kennedy for her approval. When Rose was actually confronted with the fact that the marriage plans were serious, she was stunned. She mentioned the differences in religion and the possible problems that Onassis might have with Caroline and John and their difficulties in accepting him as a stepfather. Her mind and thoughts were "awhirl" as she would later describe them.

Eventually she sorted out the difficulties and came to a decision. She wrote of that moment in her autobiography, *Times to Remember*:

"And with contemplation, it seemed to me the first basic fact was that Jackie deserved a full life, a happy future. Jack had been gone for five years, thus she had had plenty of time to think things over. She was not a person who would jump rashly into anything as important as this, so she must have her own good reasons. I decided I ought to put my doubts aside and give Jackie all the emotional support I could in what, I realized, was bound to be a time of stress for her in the weeks and months ahead. When she called I told her to make her plans as she chose to do, and to go ahead with them with my loving good wishes."

Both Jackie and Ari felt it would be better if she were not on the island when Ted arrived and while the two men talked, and as her brother-in-law was approaching the island by helicopter, Jackie was flown to Athens by seaplane and then taken by limousine to the Onassis villa in Glyfada, where she remained for a few days with Artemis.

As could be expected, Kennedy attempted to talk Onassis out of the marriage, citing the disparity of ages, Onassis' reputation with women, his maritime conflict with the U. S. government and the difficulty of being a father to John F. Kennedy's children. But the more arguments that he used to dissuade Onassis from his intentions, the more determined Onassis became. As Jorge Luis Borges has said, uncertainty is unknown to the Greeks, and to Onassis such a state was an impossibility. It was no longer a question *if* he and Jackie would marry — they had decided that months before — but when and under what financial circumstances. Dorothy Schiff, the former publisher of the *New York Post*, who had interviewed and lunched with Jackie on a number of occasions around that time, said in her biography, *Men, Money and Magic*, that Jackie's loneliness was the key factor in her wanting to marry Onassis and that "Jackie wanted to marry Onassis more than Onassis wanted to marry Jackie." Mrs. Schiff also stated that Jackie said that she thought men over sixty were often more attractive than younger men and cited General Maxwell Taylor as being "marvelous and lean." She had told her friend, ex-football star, Roosevelt Grier, that she considered marrying Onassis, "Because I was lonely and wanted someone to care about me and someone I could care about and there was no more John Kennedy." Ted Kennedy had, on Jackie's behalf and with her knowledge, discussed her financial situation with several of her lawyers and acted as her spokesman. He suggested a marriage contract spelling out all of the details and Onassis agreed.

Lawyers working in New York for both Jackie and Ari conferred privately, by phone, with their clients—and in Jackie's case with both her and Ted Kennedy—and in a relatively short time, drew up a contract that was mutually acceptable. Kennedy laughed out loud when he quipped: "Now remember, Ari, no invisible ink on this one." Onassis guffawed. Although the document was concerned with many millions of dollars and ranged over a number of highly personal and intimate areas that had nothing to do with money, Jackie and Ari never once directly discussed it together.

Working in Athens, Onassis' secretary, Lynn Alpha, typed the first draft of the contract and then flew to New York and personally delivered it to Jackie's financial adviser, Andre Meyer, whose offices are in the Carlyle Hotel.

Meyer conferred with her and then made specific proposals to Ari's lawyers, who would, in turn, discuss them with Onassis. Except for minor changes of words, or intent, Onassis made few additions or deletions to the agreement after it was appended and changed by Meyer. The 173-clause marriage contract between Aristotle Onassis and Jacqueline Kennedy has never been made public, but a former employee of Onassis, Christian Cafarakis, did see a copy of it shortly after it had been drawn up and described some of its details:

- Jackie was to receive a $3 million "payment" in tax-free bonds.
- Jackie was not required to give Onassis a child.

176

- The couple agreed that they need only spend Catholic holidays and summer vacations together. The rest of their time could be spent alone, wherever they so chose.
- Separate bedrooms had to be provided whenever they were together.
- If Onassis decided to leave his wife, he must automatically give her $10 million for each year of their marriage.
- If Jackie decided to leave her husband before five years of marriage, she'd receive only $20 million in total. If she left him after five years, she would have received $20 million, in addition to a trust fund of $180,000 for the ten years thereafter.
- If Onassis died when Jackie was still his wife, she was to receive $100 million.
- If Jackie died before her husband, all of her property and money would go to John and Caroline, and they would be supported by Onassis until they were 21 years of age.
- If both Jackie and Ari died before their children, the children would be entrusted to Prince and Princess Radziwill.
- The children received $5,000 a month each for education, clothing, nurses, medical bills and pocket money.
- All expenses, averaging $10,000 a month, pertaining to Jackie's New York apartment and the maintainence of her automobiles were paid directly by Onassis.
- Jackie's medical expenses, hairdressers, cosmeticians, etc., averaging $7,000 a month, would be paid.
- $10,000 a month was allowed Jackie for the purchase of new clothing.
- $6,000 a month was allowed her for a staff of personal bodyguards.

On October 17, Mrs. Hugh D. Auchincloss, Jackie's mother, made the announcement that her daughter was about to be married to Aristotle Onassis. Twelve hours later, in Athens, Onassis' sister Artemis announced his plans to marry on Skorpios, stating that her family "was extremely happy over the match."

Jackie was in New York and Onassis in Athens when the news was flashed around the globe. One of Jackie's friends, author Truman Capote, gave a short comment to the press, from his apartment in Brooklyn: "I've known for six months that they were going to be married. Harlech never pretended to be anything more than a friend." Newsmen gathered outside Jackie's apartment in an unsuccessful attempt to get an interview or statement, while the presence of Onassis at the Grand Bretagne Hotel in downtown Athens—he had been having a drink with a friend in the lounge—caused a near riot of newsmen, photographers and gapers, who congregated on the street outside of the hotel. Onassis answered two questions, thrown to him by the press, "She accepted my proposal by telephone. I've just come from having a physical checkup and my doctor says I'm in perfect health. Yes, it is true, I'm marrying her tomorrow or within three days at the latest. I can't say exactly when because I must first see and talk to her." When asked about a honeymoon, he replied: "We'll have it on Skorpios unless Jackie wants to take a tour of the Mediterranean with *Christina*." He then said, "I have so many family problems in my head to settle, please leave me alone now and give me your blessings." Privately, Onassis scoffed at the remark made in one of the American papers that the impending marriage was merely a financial-social relationship. Jackie was to be his wife, *ardently*, he insisted, and he was to be her *appetent* husband. He left by a rear entrance and his limousine took him to Glyfada.

In order to get a marriage license, Onassis' lawyer had to take a helicopter to the Lefkas diocese of the Greek Orthodox Church and present evidence of Onassis' divorce from Tina. The U. S. Consulate in Athens was also contacted and had to produce formal notification of John F. Kennedy's death. The document, properly translated into Greek, also stated that to the best of its knowledge, Jacqueline Kennedy was not committing bigamy.

In deciding to marry on his privately-owned island of Skorpios, in what was already being described as the wedding of the century, it is possible that Onassis remembered — and wanted to avoid — the media circus that accompanied the marriage of his former friends, Prince Rainier and Grace Kelly. Although, Jackie and Ari were commoners in fact, the public attached royal significance to the union. Rainier had said about his marriage, afterwards, that because of all the motion picture cameras, photographers and newsmen, he couldn't "see" or enjoy his own wedding and that it would have been better "if we were married in a small chapel in the mountains somewhere."

The tiny white-washed, neoclassic Chapel of Pan-iyitsa (Little Virgin) on Skorpios, where Jackie and Ari were married, sat on a high knoll in a grove of stately cypress trees. From the courtyard of the chapel, it was possible to see the *Christina* sitting in the harbor below, a beehive of activity in preparation for the reception following the wedding.

The privacy that Jackie and Ari thought they were assuring themselves by having the wedding on a remote Ionian Island was not to be, however. Reporters and photographers from all over the world gathered at the nearby fishing village of Nidri, planning a barrage of press coverage of the wedding on Skorpios. Jackie was adamant, it has been reported, that no newsmen be allowed anywhere near the island. Onassis ingeniously organized his own security forces of patrol boats, reinforced by boats and helicopters of the Greek Navy, to keep the horde of pressmen a minimum of 1,100 yards away from the island.

When a helicopter, hired by a group from the press, ventured too close to the island, they were warned off by two larger choppers, using electric megaphones. At another point, before the wedding began, Achilleus Kapsambellis, Onassis' security chief, punched one of the photographers who managed to land on the island. As a consequence, a flotilla of fishing boats, hired by the press, attempted to "invade" the island in a protest landing. They were prevented from doing so

179

by the more than 200 security guards hired expressly for that purpose.

Finally, Jackie released a statement to the besiegers:

"We know you understand that even though people may be well-known, they still hold in their hearts the emotions of a simple person for the moments that are the most important of those we know on earth — birth, marriage and death. We wish our wedding to be a private moment in the little chapel among the cypresses of Skorpios with only members of the family present, five of them little children. If you will give us those moments, we will so gladly give you all the cooperation possible for you to take the pictures you need."

Finally, peace was restored, the newsmen backed off and the ceremony began. A light rain began to fall, the trees began to droop, the weather chilled and the chapel was illuminated by many candles. Jackie was dressed in a white mini-skirted dress with a lace top, which had been designed by Valentino in Rome. Onassis was dressed in his typical blue suit and white shirt, but for the occasion sported a red tie. Both bride and groom wore sprays of orange blossoms. Onassis was in front of the chapel when Jackie arrived and they kissed each other on both cheeks.

Only 25 people could fit in the chapel and aside from the bride and groom, there were Jackie and Ari's sons and daughters, John and Caroline and Alexander and Christina; Onassis' sisters and their husbands, Jackie's sister, Lee, and her husband, the two Kennedy sisters-in-law Pat and Jean, Jackie's mother and stepfather and a small number of Onassis' close friends and business associates.

The starkly-simple ceremony was performed by Father Polykorpos Athanasias, the pastor of the Kapnikarea Church in central Athens. The century-old ritual was pre-scribed by Greek Orthodox tradition. A small chorus sang Byzantine hymns throughout the ceremony.

The priest chanted in Greek while the couple stood, hand in hand, both crowned with white orange blossoms, a symbol of purity and fertility. The high point came when the priest raised the gold-encased New Testament and both bride and groom, in turn, kissed it. The priest then said, first in Greek and then in English: "The servant of God, Aristotle, is wedlocked to the servant of God, Jacqueline, in the name of the Father, the Son and the Holy Ghost, Amen." The couple then exchanged rings, both rings first being put on Ari's finger and then both on Jackie's and finally one on each. Jackie's eyes misted over at this point and she came near to fully crying. They then did the dance of Isaiah three times around the altar; Jackie and Ari did a slow prance, while everyone gathered closely around and threw flower petals at them, while they tried to perform the custom of attempting to step on each other's feet. According to Greek superstition, whoever steps first on the other's foot is guaranteed the dominant role in the marriage.

The only definite way that most of the newsmen were to actually know whether the wedding took place was by watching the skies for the helicopter which was to transport the officiating priest back to the mainland—vaguely reminiscent of the populace watching for the black or white smoke announcing the election of a new Pope.

As a wedding gift, Onassis gave Jackie a pair of heart-shaped ruby earrings and a huge matching ring. The cost was approximately $1 million.

The reaction to the marriage by the "world at large" was one of incredulousness. Stockholm's *Expressen* asked, "Jackie, how could you?" French political commentator Andre Fontaine wrote in *Le Monde*; "Jackie, whose staunch courage during John's funeral made such an impression, now chooses to shock by marrying a man who could be her father and whose career contradicts—rather strongly, to say the least—the liberal spirit that animated President Kennedy." Even Callas made a statement, dipped in acid: "First I lost my weight, then I lost my voice, now I lost Onassis. Jackie was smart to give a grandfather to her children."

In the United States, most people were critical of the marriage and an actual group of protesters, complete with signs and picket line, met in front of Jackie's New York apartment, ignoring the fact that she wasn't there. It was the end of

Camelot for many Americans, claiming that Jackie had crossed the line of propriety by marrying a man old enough to be her father; marrying a man not of her faith; marrying a man of another nationality. If Jackie *had* to marry a foreigner, most Americans hoped it would have been English aristocrat Lord Harlech. Even the differences in their sizes was brought up in and out of the press. Onassis was five feet five inches in height, Jackie five feet eight inches without heels, which she usually wore. "A woman needs a man, not a radiator cap," hissed one of Jackie's friends. Onassis himself commented on the height difference, "I've always been attracted to tall, statuesque women. I guess I should have been a sculptor."

Only in Greece was the marriage "accepted" by the general public and "Jackie fever" spread throughout the larger cities. One Greek newspaper, *Acropolis*, stated: "The wedding will bring Greece to the forefront in a manner no one could have dreamed." Most Greeks felt proud that one of their countrymen married the former First Lady of the United States. Tired of the political strife of the 18-month rule of the military junta, the Greeks were hungry for some romance to discuss. They also considered the marriage to have great political overtones, and that Jackie's arrival "as one of them" would contribute to the bolstering of the return to parliamentary rule. Greek people in the small villages and island towns had a somewhat different view of the marriage than their compatriots in the cities, however. In Greek custom, women meekly accept that with marriage they belong to their husbands, not only to death, but forever more. In the Greek countryside and still primitive towns, a widow remains in mourning, wears black and is not expected to marry for the rest of her life. A number of Greek countryfolk frowned on the marriage for that reason. They believed that Jackie should have remained faithful to J.F.K.'s memory.

Aside from the international tongue wagging, the theology of the marriage caused real concern to Jackie and Ari. As a Roman Catholic, Jackie was not permitted to marry a divorced man, and in times past she would have automatically been excommunicated the moment she was married. The Greek Orthodox religion, at least tokenly followed by Onassis, permitted its followers to marry three times. Cardinal Cushing, who had performed her first marriage to J.F.K. fifteen years before she wed Onassis, was criticized himself for "allowing" Jackie to marry Onassis. The old man went on television and with his broad, Irish-Boston accent, defended her, "My advice to people is to stop criticizing the poor woman. She has had an enormous amount of sadness in her life and deserves what happiness she can find." And then with an air of mystery said that she had told him things, in confidence, that had international implications. "Nobody would believe me if I said what I know," said Cushing. Immediately, speculation began to grow that Onassis might be named Premier of Greece and that Jackie would be First Lady again, but of another country.

The attacks on Cushing were so plentiful and forceful that he made an official offer to the Vatican to resign his post as Cardinal of Boston. It was not accepted.

To confuse the situation even further, spokesmen for the Greek Orthodox Church stated that the patriarchate of Istanbul, the Supreme Orthodox Church authority, had come to an agreement with the Vatican before the wedding took place and received assurances from the Pope that the marriage would be approved. The Vatican neither affirmed nor denied it.

Finally, a statement came from the Vatican that "Mrs. Kennedy," as she was still referred to, must be considered to be in a state of mortal sin. In the Catholic religion, a mortal sin can be cancelled — or forgiven — if it is told in confession, if the sinner is truly sorry for having committed the offense and if penance for the sin is practiced. After a short while had passed, Jackie continued to receive the sacraments of the Catholic Church, so it can be assumed that the proper action on her part was taken. Soon, the entire religion matter was forgotten and dropped as quickly as it was brought up.

13

Standing on the terrace of Jackie's Fifth Avenue apartment, Onassis watched the sun go down behind Central Park. He had been ready at six—for cocktails—but Jackie still continued to dress and coif in her bedroom. He busied himself around the apartment and had a few drinks alone. He was annoyed.

Jackie had still not appeared when the first guest arrived. It was Frank Sinatra. Onassis had never met him, but they relaxed with each other, speaking Italian, establishing and continuing a rapport that lasted for the remainder of the evening.

Soon, the Duchins, the Lerners, the Paleys, the Bernsteins, and assorted other guests began to assemble. All were either discreetly disturbed or flattered by the legion of photographers that had gathered downstairs in an attempt to get pictures of the attendees of one of New York's most chic dinner parties.

The caterer from La Cote Basque began to worry that the evening was beginning to run late; the quality of the *souffle au fraise* with champagne would be impossible to predict.

Jackie drifted into her own party at slightly past eight-thirty, dressed in a long, yellow silk gown, just minutes before the guests of honor arrived—New York's Mayor and Mrs. John Lindsay.

After re-introductions all around, the guests entered the dining room.

Onassis' goldfish-bowl marriage to Jackie was a strange and strained relationship, with just a few pleasant interludes at the very beginning.

Alexander and Christina Onassis were both openly opposed to their father's new match, and Onassis had to plead with them to attend the wedding. They came, but their feelings were only thinly disguised. One story reported that Alexander agreed to come to the wedding only if his father would in turn agree to stop criticizing his relationship with Baroness Fiona von Thyssen, and stop objecting to his flying his own planes. According to the story, Onassis relented and agreed to both demands. On the day of the wedding, Alexander told the press, "My father needed a wife but I certainly didn't need a stepmother." Later, in a more relaxed mood, he said: "I do not understand my father's fascination for the Kennedy woman. He's been in love with her for ages. She's beautiful, intelligent, and quite formidable, in the best European sense. But she can be so alarmingly exigent. She could undermine everything. She could jeopardize a whole epoch."

Christina, somber and quiet, would not speak with the press. But she was heard to refer to Jackie as "my father's unhappy compulsion."

For almost a year before the wedding, Onassis' children had been secretly hoping for and attempting to manipulate his remarriage to Tina. It had seemed a viable possibility. They loved both their mother and their father and had always dreamed that the initial schism could be repaired. Onassis had been incensed at Tina's remarriage. Tina could not abide his publicity-strident relationship with Callas; still, there were signs that they had still loved each other when they divorced, and still loved each other eight years later. Christina and Alexander had been at odds for years with Callas and she with them. "Maria never liked me very much," Christina once said. "She even used to accuse me of trying to separate her from my father, which was untrue, of course."

Onassis was not unaware of his children's plans to promote another attempt at marriage with Tina; indeed, whenever they brought up the subject of Maria Callas, whom they disliked, the implication was always made by Onassis that he would never marry again, because he was "still faithful" to Tina — at least in his respect for their previous marriage vows. And, in fact, he did not marry Callas. Instead, he married Jacqueline Kennedy.

Only days after their wedding, Onassis flew by helicopter to Athens to discuss the biggest financial negotiations of his career. Headlines in Greek papers blared: "Onassis leaves Jackie during honeymoon . . . to talk business."

Onassis' newest business deal was an attempt to pour over $400 million into Greece in an attempt to not only bolster the economy, but to forge Greece into an industrial nation. The investment package would have included a new oil refinery, an aluminum plant, scores of light industries, a shipyard, an underground air terminal in Athens, and a string of tourist resorts and hotels spread along the Aegean and Ionian. Not only was the proposal the largest business transaction ever suggested by Onassis, it was the single largest economic undertaking in Greek history.

It became apparent that as one of the richest men in the world, Onassis had a drive to accumulate more than anyone — except he — could want. He explained it this way: "It's not a question of money. After you reach a certain point, money becomes unimportant. What matters is success. The sensible thing would be for me to stop now. But I can't. I have to keep aiming higher and higher — just for the thrill."

Immediately, Onassis fell under great criticism, especially from the United States press, for wanting to become the public partner of the dictatorial regime of the Greek junta.

Onassis had originally proposed to Greece's Premier George Papadopoulos the building of a $60 million oil refinery, a deal that would assure him a new and committed customer for his fleet of tankers.

The Greek colonels knew that Onassis could invest more in their country, and they agreed to give approval for building the refinery, only if Onassis would agree to build a $250 million aluminum smelting plant as well. Onassis not only agreed to the aluminum plant proposal, but suggested that he construct a thermoelectric power plant to utilize the waste gases from the oil refinery as a source of power for the aluminum smelter.

The negotiations temporarily broke down over the issue of the power plant because electrical power is a state monopoly in Greece and the Athens government would not relinquish its right to a private corporation, no matter what the price. The junta also asked Onassis to transfer the registration of a sizable portion of his 100-ship tanker fleet from Liberia to Greece. In addition, some of the colonels were demanding bribes, and although Onassis was not averse to such a method of doing business, the amounts they were asking for were, even to Onassis, exorbitant. He refused them.

The talks continued, and the $400 million investment looked like it might become as much as $600 million — or even $700 million to cover all the plans that both Onassis and the government cared to initiate. A second, and then even a third oil refinery were discussed. Onassis attempted to interest a group of Japanese companies, almost all of them in heavy industry, to form a consortium to invest in the various projects. But until such time as the details of Onassis' negotiations could be settled, the Japanese would not commit themselves and the Greek government stated that "They . . . would not be influenced by the possible participation of the Japanese and the influx of their money."

Niarchos also submitted plans and bids concerning the concessions; the government quietly sat back to study

187

them. Not only did Niarchos propose to do everything that Onassis said he would do, but Niarchos was willing to put in more of his own money to do it. A great part of Onassis' money would have come from foreign interests, in some cases from sources not particularly approved of by the Greek colonels.

The Niarchos-Onassis rivalry for the government contract was used by the Papadopoulos government, which played one man against the other — just as the Karamanlis regime, ten years before, had taken advantage of their unreasoning competitiveness. The result of that contest had been Onassis' assumption of control over Olympic Airways and Niarchos' control over Skaramanga shipyards. The only difference this time was the size of the transaction involved. Whoever could secure this new package would gain the virtual economic control of the country.

Eventually, the government and Onassis reached a tentative agreement to go ahead. Niarchos was furious and attacked on two fronts simultaneously, using a combination of honey and venom. He offered the financially ailing Greek state a loan of $100 million, with very low interest, for a period of twenty years — a highly attractive proposition for the cash-poor nation. Next, he called a press conference stating that the reasons his original bids had been ignored were due to "irregularities" that had taken place between Onassis and certain government officials, and that Onassis had misrepresented facts in his proposal which would cause the state to lose $150 million if they went through with the deal. Within 24 hours, the government canceled its tentative contract with Onassis and announced that it would consider new bids up to July of 1969.

Onassis called Niarchos' criticisms "Nonsense. They do not respond to reality."

The Niarchos accusation revolved around the amount of money to be paid for each ton of crude oil to be carried in Onassis' ships. According to Niarchos, Onassis had promised to pay $14 per ton, when in actuality, he would have only paid $11.50.

Niarchos was promised the contract when he offered a much lower rate per ton for crude oil; he also deposited a

$20 million letter of credit — on account — at an Athens bank.

When Onassis visited the United States just days before the cut-off date, he secretly met with President Richard Nixon aboard the presidential yacht *Julie* then docked off Grand Key Island. Whether the visit was purely social or for business or political reasons is not known, but Niarchos attempted to make the visit appear sinister, accusing Onassis of "exploiting the Nixon visit" in his attempt to secure the contract.

With both Niarchos and Onassis constantly at each other's throats, the Greek government continued to stall for time. The denouement of one of Europe's most ambitious financial deals was bizarre.

Onassis was asked to deposit certain monies — as had Niarchos — as a guarantee of his interest. He refused and never renegotiated the contract, and after the fall of the junta, Niarchos withdrew his bids. Finally, no new industrial revolution ever took place in Greece.

Shortly after they were married, Ari and Jackie flew to England where Jackie stayed at Lee Radziwill's mansion Turville Grange, near Henley-on-Thames, and Onassis ensconced himself at his suite at Claridge's in London. As Onassis talked business each day — he was attempting to negotiate a new tanker — Jackie and Lee spent time talking and walking Lee's dogs in the countryside. In the evening Jackie and Ari would meet for dinner.

The question of how the "marriage of the century" would progress and how it was faring, almost day by day, became one of the favorite topics of newspapers, magazines and gossip columnists around the world, and both Jackie and Ari seemed to be playing, very consciously, into the hands of the media, in attempting to prove that they had an open and uninhibited marriage.

He was seen having dinner at Maxim's in Paris with actress Elsa Martinelli, and even with Maria Callas. Ari suggested to both Callas and Jackie that they meet. Callas was agreeable, but Jackie didn't want it for numerous reasons; she felt she did not have to elaborate why. When asked about the

189

possible meeting, by a journalist, Callas replied: "It is not wanted by the other side."

Although that meeting failed, Onassis engineered another. Once and for a wonder, he attempted to put his past troubles behind him and invited Niarchos and Tina to dine with him and Jackie at Maxim's. Everyone accepted, and according to a friend who was invited to have drinks afterward, the foursome shared a superficially pleasant evening together.

Onassis also arranged dinner parties for himself and Jackie with Rose Kennedy, whom he took to calling "Rosie," much to the amusement of Jackie. When the threesome went to dine, usually in Paris, often Ari and Rose would sit in the back seat of his limousine, while Jackie sat up front with the chauffeur. Onassis charmed Rose Kennedy into sharing Parisian night life with them, and on at least one occasion she even accompanied them to *Open One*, where like everyone else, she took a place at the low tables and sprawled on the floor atop multi-colored pillows.

In New York Jackie continued to appear at concerts and society functions, "escorted" by the men she had been seeing before she married Onassis. He immediately explained the arrangement to all the eyebrow-raisers:

"Jackie is a little bird that needs its freedom as well as its security, and she gets them both from me. She can do exactly as she pleases — visit international fashion shows and travel and go out with friends to the theater or anyplace. And I, of course, will do exactly as I please. I never question her and she never questions me."

In fact, their marriage, at least at the beginning, was relatively conventional except for the long separations usually initiated by Onassis for business reasons — never for anything else. He was, in fact, a jealous husband, and if a photograph of Jackie appeared, showing her giving a slightly intimate look to another man, he would call from any part of the world and complain. And although she was more liberal concerning his exploits, she once tearfully flew to Paris on the spur of the

190

moment, two hours after *The New York Post* published a picture taken the night before of Onassis and Callas dining at Maxim's. Ari was reputedly contrite, and he and Jackie spent an idyllic weekend on the town and touring the French countryside.

From the very first summer after Jackie and Ari were married, John and Caroline spent every long school vacation on Skorpios. Often they were allowed and encouraged to bring one or more friends along to keep them company; Onassis always paid all expenses, although he was careful to ensure that his new family and their guests flew on Olympic Airways planes.

Onassis purchased a variety of horses and ponies and had them brought to the island so the children could ride them. He also presented John and Caroline with a sleek, red, 28-foot sailing boat, just for their private use. Caroline christened it *Caroline*. So that John wouldn't feel hurt, Onassis presented him with a red speedboat with the name "John" printed on it.

That first summer together, 1969, was a period of growth for Jackie and Ari. It was really the first long, uninterrupted time that they had ever spent together with Caroline and John. The children had come with Jackie for the Christmas holidays the previous winter, but had only spent a little over a week in Greece. It rained most of the time, and they had spent all of the holiday sightseeing in museums in Athens—sometimes quite crankily (although they made it to the Acropolis, willingly, even in the rain)—and aboard the *Christina*, which was docked at Glyfada.

On Skorpios during that long, peaceful summer, the informality and privacy calmed everyone. Onassis took an immense liking to the nine-year-old John, and spent hours with him, walking and jeeping over the island and showing the boy everything on the yacht that he was interested in. On occasion, Onassis even took him to Athens by seaplane when his business called him there. While Onassis conducted his affairs, John would tour Athens or go to a movie, accompanied, of course, by the inevitable security guard.

Onassis loved Jackie. Being with her did not produce

any new set of unfamiliar emotions; rather, it revived and concentrated all the affections he had known in the past. He wanted to please her in every way, and he showered her with gifts — jewelry, gowns, furs, entertainments. He lived the role of Aladdin and his lamp, and he enjoyed it. Fred Sparks wrote an entire book based on Jackie and Ari's first year of marriage, and he claimed that they spent over $20 million in that one year. Even if this figure is greatly inflated, millions of dollars were spent, and much of it to fulfill Jackie's desires.

Throughout the summer, Onassis usually had to fly to Athens once each week, and he occasionally made trips elsewhere. While he was gone, Jackie rested, sunbathed, and read voraciously. One day, toward the end of July, she exchanged her constant book for the small portable television set aboard the *Christina*. There, she and the children gathered excitedly to watch the successful splashdown of the Apollo II, as it returned from the moon. Onassis didn't get to see it; he was in Athens that day, wrapped in a heated discussion with government officials about the oil refinery.

A few days later, July 28, was Jackie's fortieth birthday. Onassis wanted orchids flown to Skorpios, but could find none in all of Athens, so he settled for twelve dozen red roses. He also presented her with a diamond necklace, bracelet, and earrings and a forty-carat diamond ring worth $1 million. One of Greece's top jewelers, Ilias Lalaounis of the famed firm of Zolotas, who had sold Onassis literally millions in jewels and accessories over the years, also presented a pair of earrings to Jackie for her birthday. They looked like two hanging globes, and they represented a jeweled moon, suspended from jeweled spaceships. Studded with diamonds and rubies, the unexpected gift was as unique as it was beautiful.

That night, in the little quay of Skorpios, the *Christina* sat emblazoned with lights as a small party was held for Jackie.

A few days later, Jackie and Ari flew to Glyfada for a post-birthday family dinner and a nine-month marriage anniversary party. At about midnight, Onassis insisted that the party, which consisted of his daughter Christina, then eighteen, his two sisters and their husbands, and a number of close friends, go to the Neraida night club, a seafront bistro on the Saronic Gulf. Jackie had let slip that other than the small outdoor cafe in Nidri, just opposite Skorpios, she had never been in an actual Greek nightclub. Onassis wanted her to experience some Athenian nightlife, and the group was driven to the club in their limousines. It was an open-air restaurant and the weather was balmy, the night like velvet.

Jackie loved the *bouzouki* music and clapped, with Onassis, to the rhythm of the *syrtaki*, the dance made famous in the film *Zorba, The Greek*. Onassis was thoroughly familiar with it—he had danced it in Smyrna as a young man —its origins are Turkish, rather than Greek.

Onassis explained all the complicated steps to all the dances, and although she didn't attempt any of them, she professed her desire to learn them, together with "every word of those beautiful songs."

Sometimes they talked alone, softly, and he kept his arm around her protectively and with affection. She seemed to enjoy the closeness, and they kissed several times. But the mood was mostly gay and laughing. Onassis taught her a few Greek phrases, and at one point, she stood, raised her glass and toasted first the musicians, and then her party, in Greek. She beamed for the entire evening, and Onassis' friends claim that they had never seen him so variously proud, cavalier, felicitous and captivated.

When dawn began to break, everyone started to go home, but Jackie and Ari remained—he paid the musicians extra to keep playing.

It was close to nine in the morning when they finally left, Onassis high and rumpled, and Jackie—maybe for the first time in her adult life—without lipstick in public.

Onassis' celebrityhood, after his marriage to Jackie, surpassed the boundaries of even the very famous. The public began to take an abnormal interest in his comings and goings, his life-style in general. Speculation about him became an almost daily pastime in newspapers throughout the world. Articles and biographies about him were not enough. A life as fabulous and unbelievable as his seemed more closely related to fiction. As a result, Aristotle Onassis soon became the apparent model for the protagonist of a number of novels. His name wasn't used, some authors even claimed that their books could in no way be considered *roman a clefs*, that they did not portray any real characters, living or dead. Nonetheless, it was impossible to ignore the similarities between the fictional accounts and the realities of Onassis' life.

Pierre Rey, in his novel, *The Greek*, talks of a Greek shipping magnate named Socrates Satrapoulos, who happened to own a private, exotic island called Serpentella. It is, of course, the story of Skorpios, down to the smallest details. Here is Rey's description of that "imaginary" island:

"The island of Serpentella was the private property of Socrates Satrapoulos. When he had bought it several years earlier, everyone had laughed. Even Satrapoulos, they said, could not turn this stretch of barren rock into anything but what the gods had always intended it to be—the home of snakes, scorpions, and spiders. But Satrapoulos possessed power such as the dwellers on Olympus had never dreamed. At the touch of his checkbook, an army of horticulturists, engineers, land-scapers, and architects had descended upon Serpentella. For months, bulldozers had worked to level some parts of the island and to create hills and valleys on others. Thousands of tons of good earth had been brought by ship, and this had been followed by shiploads of flowers and lemon, orange, olive, and eucalyptus trees. But, before any planting had been done, the entire island was doused with enormous quantities of pesticides and insecticides, so that now one might search in vain for a single snake, scorpion, or spider, to say nothing of mosquitoes. A few colonies of ants were the only form of animal life tolerated by the two hundred people whose sole function it was to see to the comfort of the master of this artificial paradise."

Sidney Sheldon, in *The Other Side of Midnight* (which was also made into a motion picture), describes the island of Constantin Demaris, this way:

194

"The island was inaccessible except by helicopter and yacht, and both the airfield and the private harbor were patrolled twenty-four hours a day by armed guards with trained German shepherds. The island was Constantin Demaris' private domain, and no one intruded without an invitation. Over the years, its visitors had included kings and queens, presidents and ex-presidents, movie stars, opera singers and famous writers and painters. They had all come away awed. Constantin Demaris was the third wealthiest and one of the most powerful men in the world, and he had taste and style and knew how to spend his money to create beauty."

Jacqueline Susann, in her novel *Dolores*, wrote about the beautiful and fashionable widow of an assassinated American president who married Baron Erik de Savornee, an Onassis-like character who had " . . . vast holdings in the Near and Middle East . . . was built like a prizefighter and was known to have been in many a brawl on the docks. Yet he also owned many luxury hotels throughout the world and an art collection worth billions."

And Nicholas Gage's portrait of Onassis in *The Bourlotas Fortune* was probably the most thinly disguised of all, really a fictional biography of another Greek shipowner, where Demosthenes Militas—Onassis—is quoted as saying, "Ever since I was a schoolboy in Smyrna, I've dreamed of owning a ship."

A motion picture, *The Greek Tycoon*, which began filming in the summer of 1977, resembled the life of Onassis. Anthony Quinn was secured to play the title role. "Onassis was convinced that a movie would eventually be made about him," said Quinn. "He was just concerned that it was portrayed accurately. He actually expressed hope that I would play him in a film. I was flattered."

In the summer of 1971, Onassis' daughter, Christina, then twenty, shocked her father by marrying a 47-year-old real-estate broker from Los Angeles, Joseph Bolker. Aside from her not asking his permission, Onassis was incensed for another reason: Bolker was Jewish, and Onassis was concerned over the possibilities of a rupture with his oil connections as a result of "guilt by association."

Onassis cut off all communication with his daughter, but not before he first threatened to cut off Christina's multimillion dollar trust fund if she did not divorce Bolker. Finally, after nine months, the couple separated, but for other reasons, as cited by Christina: "I did not want to be separated from my family. Mr. Bolker's work keeps him in Los Angeles. I must live in Greece."

Another blow to Onassis at that time, although financial rather than emotional, was his failed attempt to buy out Harland and Wolff, a huge Belfast shipping company. He owned 26 percent of the company. After over a year of negotiation, the government of Northern Ireland decided that since it had invested over $50 million in keeping the company solvent, it should remain under Irish control. Onassis had nothing to say about the future of the company and was bought out for $250,000, a sum greatly less than he had originally paid for his shares.

In New York, it was rumored early in the 1970s that Onassis and Jackie had already begun to drift apart. As the stories went, Jackie spent more and more time in the United States, and whenever Onassis came to New York, he was forced to stay at the Hotel Pierre, simply because Jackie didn't want him to stay at her apartment. That story is untrue. Actually, it was not until much later that the marriage began to manifest signs of strain.

Onassis kept a "transient" suite at the Hotel Pierre — although to him it was permanent — for tax purposes. If his "permanent" address were the same as Jackie's, he would have made himself vulnerable to some enormous tax problems, and avoiding taxes was almost a religion to Onassis. It was important, therefore, not only that he disclaim Jackie's apartment as partly his own, it was equally important, for financial reasons, that he not "live" there. Since he paid not one penny in U. S. taxes, his name could not appear on any leases and therefore arrangements were made for Jackie to be the leaseholder in a new apartment atop Onassis' Olympic Towers on Fifth Avenue.

Actually, although it was not generally known, he *did* live in Jackie's apartment most of the time he was in New York. A small room was kept for him, and it contained a supply of his clothing and personal effects. (Onassis refused to travel with suitcases. To avoid such inconveniences, he had his staff stock each of his many homes with whatever clothing, toiletry articles, shoes, and so on that he might need when staying in that country.)

He only stayed at the Pierre on those evenings that he had to conduct business, or when he knew he would have to work through the night, making calls, arguing prices, sending messages by courier, and generally supervising much activity. Jackie usually retired early, and her apartment house was not nearly as well equipped as the Pierre to serve Onassis' business needs. It is also true that on those evenings that Onassis went clubbing with friends, he also went straight to the Pierre rather than disturb Jackie's household at four A.M.

Jackie and Ari's marriage still seemed vibrant as late as the fall of 1972, when as a surprise for Ari, Jackie gave a lush champagne party for sixty guests at *El Morocco*, to celebrate their fourth wedding anniversary. One guest observed that they seemed enormously at ease with each other, "a lot cozier than I had expected."

A few other guests observed something wrong, however, although not between the hostess and host. Ari seemed tired, depressed, perhaps not in good health. Jackie was physically solicitous toward him, and he appreciated her concern and affection. It was soon after that evening that he received what was to him the cruelest blow of his life.

14

"Above all, Alexandros loved the skies and flying. He became a perfect pilot in only three or four years. I have never seen a more careful, meticulous pilot. He also used his abilities to good ends. He had carried out a number of mercy missions. I, as a father, never stopped him from doing these things. He was a nice boy, a promising boy . . ."
Onassis, after his son's death.

In 1973, a worldwide inflation greatly increased the demand for more oil and Onassis' tankers were greatly in demand. A supertanker voyage from the Persian Gulf around the Cape had been commanding a price of approximately $2.5 million and within a matter of months, due to the boon, the price went up to $8 million, or even more, for a single trip. By the end of the year, Onassis had made a clear profit of over $100 million, perhaps the best single year of his career.

Flush with a new influx of capital, Onassis decided to expand his tanker fleet by one third, at an estimated cost of $360 million. Two of his new super-supertankers, weighing 426,000 tons each, would cost over $80 million each. Four other tankers, totalling a million tons, would cost a total of $200 million. Construction was immediately begun.

The Arab oil embargo, later in 1973, caused one of the largest depressions in the history of tanker shipping. Onassis had blundered. His new ships were not needed, and he could secure no new charters for them. He immediately cancelled further construction on the two super-supertankers and accepted a loss of $12 million. One other of the smaller ships was also cancelled at a loss of $5 million. The remaining ships were too far advanced in their construction to be stopped; Onassis began to see a disastrous financial crisis beginning to grow throughout his empire. By the end of 1974, all of his reverses reduced the total worth of his assets by about one half — from approximately $1 billion to $500 million.

But his financial losses, as depressing and humiliating as they were, were relatively mild compared to the assault upon his emotions that he was about to experience.

Ever since he was a child, Alexander Onassis had been obsessed with speed. At first he was interested in cars and as soon as he was legally able — and even before that — he pleaded with his father, successfully, to buy him a sports car, and he became a fixture in motion speeding all over the French Riviera in his Ferrari.

But if automobiles were his love, airplanes were his passion. He began taking flying lessons when he was in his teens and received his pilot's license at the age of eighteen. Even though Onassis owned an airline and personally traveled in excess of 100,000 miles a year, he was not particularly fond of flying nor did he consider it completely safe. Onassis begged Alexander to abandon his plans to buy his own private plane and tried to discourage him from flying altogether. His influence with Alexander, in this area, however, was nil.

When Onassis realized that there was no dissuading Alexander from his interest in flying, he appointed him Director of Island Services of Olympic Airways. The young man proved to be a competent executive and soon was responsible for establishing regularly scheduled helicopter, seaplane and light craft service to almost all of the Greek islands—many of them enjoyed an influx of needed tourism, as a result.

Onassis loved his son deeply. He hadn't spent very much time with him or Christina in their childhood, and there was still an awkwardness between them concerning their mother, Tina. As Alexander grew older and the two men began to explore common interests, Alexander allowed himself to relax toward his father and they enjoyed a close rapport.

Onassis did what he thought a father should do for a son. The trust fund that he had established for him and his sister in the 1950s, made them multimillionaires as soon as they became legal adults. In addition, Onassis attempted to teach Alexander everything he could about all his businesses, taking him into his most guarded confidences, revealing his deepest secrets, relating information that only Onassis himself had about his far-flung and byzantine operations. Alexander was a dedicated but slow student of his father's ways. His interest in ships was far less than that in planes, but he nevertheless accepted with seriousness the position his father had placed him in as the logical heir and eventual controller of the Onassis fortune.

Onassis attempted to school Alexander in the vagaries of pleasure, as well as business. They wined and dined together, were seen in Athens and Paris nightclubs constantly, and Onassis did what he could do to promote the image of his son, like himself, as the consummate playboy. Onassis established a bachelor apartment for Alexander when he was very young and encouraged the boy to entertain women there. Eventually, Alexander moved into a suite at the Athens Hilton. Over the years, his father introduced him to some of the most beautiful women in the world, but when Alexander fell in love on his own, with Fiona von Thyssen—a high fashion model and former German baroness famous for her extraordinarily beautiful body and her ostentatious habit of simultaneously walking her pet Japanese panther and leopard on leashes—Onassis disapproved. Knowing, however, that Alexander had a naturally rebellious side, Onassis did not protest too strongly. For fear that Alexander might do something rash just to spite him, he invited the couple to Skorpios and aboard the *Christina* and generally acted friendly toward Fiona, while subtly trying to implant in Alexander's mind that she was not the kind of woman he should be considering for a marriage partner. Alexander was not convinced, but neither was he ready for marriage in any event.

On January 27, 1973, Alexander, then 24 years old, crashed in a two-engine Piazzo light aircraft as it was about to take off at Athens airport. At first, it was thought that he had been at the controls, but it was learned later that Donald MacCusker, a private American pilot who was going to be the plane's permanent pilot, was flying it when it crashed. Also aboard was a Canadian, Donald MacGregor.

All three passengers were seriously hurt but Alexander was in the worst condition, virtually dead at the moment of impact. He was rushed to Kiffisia Hospital near Athens and immediately underwent surgery. Coincidentally, all of his family and those closest to him were out of Athens at the time of the accident. They were notified and flew to Greece from various parts of the world—Onassis, Christina, Artemis, Jackie, Fiona, Tina.

The first diagnosis was that Alexander had a severe concussion and had suffered brain damage. Another operation was performed with a team of surgeons and neurosurgeons, but the prognosis was poor, "Only a miracle will save him," said one of the doctors.

Onassis was grief-stricken when he visited Alexander's bedside. The young man's head was completely bandaged except for his eyes, which were closed, and an opening for oxygen. The entire family was overcome by the tragedy and kept a vigil by his bed all night long. Feeling impotent, Onassis said he felt like screaming but couldn't bring himself to do it.

The next day the doctors told Onassis that Alexander could only be kept alive by artificial means and then only for three or four days at maximum. Without having to consult anyone, Onassis knew what had to be done. He ordered the doctors to cease any extreme medical techniques just to keep his son alive for a day or two more. Within a matter of hours, Alexander died. Onassis' face had a look of anger, rather than sadness, when he explained his decision, "We decided it was in vain, so we gave the doctors the orders to stop. We weren't killing him. We were just letting him die. There is no question of euthanasia here. If he had lived, he would have been dead as a human being. His brain was destroyed and his features completely disfigured. Nothing could be done for him."

When Onassis returned from the hospital to his villa at Glyfada, everyone thought his heart would burst, so inconsolable was he over the loss of his son. He cried ceaselessly, and in the early hours of the next morning, he went out into the street in a daze, wandering for hours. He could not and would not control his grief, and when he returned home and saw a crowd of newsmen in front of the house, all he could mutter was, "He was a good boy, a good boy," and then wept as he stood with the members of the press.

Onassis seemed to lose all hope with the death of Alexander. Alexander *was* his hope and he said to everyone that he could see no sense in living himself. He saw himself in Alexander, and when his son died, so did he. His usual resiliency in time of tragedy, such as at the funeral of John F. Kennedy, and his natural ability to lift the spirits of others, was gone, unable to be rekindled.

Jackie tried to be a help and consolation to him, but she could do nothing. He became so disturbed, distressed and angered over his loss, that he could not even attend Alexander's funeral.

Perhaps in an attempt to show contempt for the fates, he claimed that the death could not have been caused by a mere accident, but only by murder. The plane was sabotaged, he contended. He offered a $500,000 reward to anyone who could prove that his son was murdered rather than killed accidentally. He also stated that if it could be proven, he would

202

donate an additional $333,000 to charity. A trial was held of MacCusker and MacGregor, and aside from the usual negligence charges, nothing was proven that could lead to the conclusion of sabotage. The matter was dropped.

Author Nicholas Gage wrote: "When Alexander died, Onassis' *raison d'etre* may have died with him." It had.

Just a few weeks after Alexander's death, Onassis suffered another blow. Actress Katina Paxinou, a lifelong friend, close to all the members of his family but mainly to Onassis, died of cancer in an Athens hospital.

He seemed to be aging overnight. The death of Katina tempered the problem and made him more morose. "He looks like an old man," said one of his aides. Jackie, Christina and Onassis' sisters met and discussed what to do and came up with the idea of a trip. Jackie organized a "safari" to Egypt, a country Onassis had always liked, but never had time to enjoy. He had said that someday he would like to go back there. Her idea was to get his mind off himself.

Gathering some of his closest relatives and gayest friends together, Jackie persuaded Onassis to go, which he did only reluctantly. They stayed at the best and largest suite of the Cairo Hilton, and the party took over an entire wing of the hotel. They visited the Pyramids, rode camels and toured the sights and bazaars by day and dined to the gyrations of bellydancers by night. Everyone had a marvelous excursion, and on occasion even Onassis laughed and enjoyed himself. Overall, however, he improved slightly but not markedly.

In addition to his loss of a love for life, Onassis also began to curtail—for the first time—his enormous business drive. Soon he was at odds with the Greek government over Olympic Airways. He began to hate his own airline and what it symbolized to him. Everywhere there was a memory or a shadow of Alexander. It was all too much for him to bear.

Although the government was willing to assume control of Olympic Airlines, Onassis would not agree to their assessment. Ready to sign the transfer of ownership after a value of $68 million had been appraised, he claimed fatigue. Even his own aides thought he was acting peculiarly as though his judgment had begun to slip. Eventually, he did relinquish the airline, but only after many vacillations and bureaucratic meanderings, methods unfamiliar to Onassis' style.

Suddenly, he also could no longer abide Jackie. Minor annoyances began to plague him. She was usually late for appointments and he was always precisely on time. Her lack of precision and a general inaccessibility sent him into a quiet rage and an absence of shared values and interests began to depress him. He thought she was overly permissive with her children: "I don't mind if they wear blue jeans," he complained to a friend, "but why can't they be clean jeans?" Jackie and his schedule began to clash: she was up at eight every morning, in bed often at ten every night. He usually slept until noon, but was still awake and going strong at 6 A.M. He had no interest in the theater, movies, ballet or opera, Jackie loved them all.

Jackie also insisted that he take another trip, this one to Acapulco, to commemorate the tenth anniversary of John F. Kennedy's death. It was where they had spent their honeymoon. It was a difficult pilgrimage for Onassis because its rationale was connected with death, and because it symbolized Jackie's continuing enshrinement of the memory of her late husband. It was not that Onassis did not acknowledge the immensity of the tragedy of John F. Kennedy, nor did he overlook the agony that Jackie went through afterwards, but the constant reminder began to haunt him, as though Jackie considered J. F. K. her *real* husband, Onassis merely a companion.

Jackie had other reasons for going to Acapulco and that was to look at real estate. They visited and inspected a number of splendid villas that were for sale. Onassis would not or could not agree to buy. Jackie insisted. They argued about it and continued to argue on the flight back on a private plane to New York. At one point, Onassis got up in the middle of a particularly heated exchange and moved to another part of the cabin and began to write what seemed to be letters. He wrote for several hours.

Jackie was also having money problems; she had invested $300,000 in the stock market and lost almost all of it. She suggested to Ari that he make up the loss for her, since

204

essentially, it represented most of her liquid capital. He adamantly refused to help her, pointing out that he had previously warned her against the investment, advising her to leave her money in the tax-free bonds that she had. If she needed money, he told her sarcastically, she should sell some of the millions of dollars worth of jewels that he had given her since they were married and she kept stored in vaults and safety deposit boxes around the world. He also suggested that she sell some of the paintings—Van Goghs, Picassos, El Grecos—he had given her for her Fifth Avenue apartment, comprising a large portion of his $20 million dollar collection.

Jackie also complained about her monthly allowance. It was not enough to support her burgeoning life-style, and Nancy Tuckerman, her secretary, was constantly calling Onassis' financial supervisor, Creon Brown, asking for additional funds. "Things simply can't go on this way in the house any longer," Jackie said to Ari. "That's too bad," he replied, "They'll just have to." He gave strict orders to his office not to advance her one penny over and above what she was entitled to in their marriage contract.

Another caper of Jackie's caught the attention of Onassis, and it involved a law suit. The famous *paparazzo* Ron Galella appeared to have an insatiable obsession with photographing Jackie. Wherever she went, not just in New York but seemingly anywhere in the world, Galella materialized, snapping the shutter of his Nikon. He made tens of thousands of dollars selling the photographs, and each time Jackie saw one of her photographs splashed across a tabloid or magazine, she became incensed. There were a number of incidents between them. Once, Jackie insisted that her bodyguard confiscate Galella's camera. Galella was even arrested.

Finally, Galella was taken to court by Jackie in a lawsuit for harassment and invasion of privacy. He countersued her for interfering with his right to make a living.

During that time, Onassis met Galella on the street and said, "I hear you're suing my wife. Maybe we can settle this for a couple of thousand dollars."

Galella told him he would talk to his lawyers and eventually asked Onassis for $100,000, an amount that Onassis refused to pay claiming it was too high, adding: "Publicity is like rain. When you're soaking wet, what difference does a few drops more make." Galella was convinced, however, that Onassis wanted to settle out of court but that Jackie would not permit it, "on principle."

Jackie won a minor victory as the court ruled that in the future, Galella could only take pictures of her and her family beyond a 50-yard radius. Onassis, however, was the loser as he was presented with the legal expenses — over $200,000. After a skirmish of haggling with the law firm that handled the case, he settled with them and paid the bill, but he never agreed with Jackie's insistence on fighting it out rather than settling it and saving a great deal of money.

In 1974, Onassis developed a disease called myasthenia gravis, a neurological disorder which manifests itself by a weakening of the muscles, most noticeably the muscles that control the upper eyelids. He began to take massive doses of cortisone to arrest it. As the disease progressed, his lids began to droop badly enough so that it interfered with his vision. The only way to keep them open was to tape them. His doctors showed him how to use a transparent, colorless tape, pressing it close to the eyebrow and carrying it carefully down to the upper eyelid. If done properly, the tape would have been barely visible. But the procedure took quite a few minutes, and Onassis grew impatient standing in front of a mirror that long, fussing with his appearance. He switched to surgical or adhesive tape; it was much more noticeable, and sometimes he plastered a piece in place so quickly that the end of the tape hung over the edge of his lashes. But it did the job, and it took much less of the time that was so important to him.

He was sensitive about his occasionally odd appearance, though. Sometimes he taped only one eye open, to give the other a rest, but he looked so peculiar, then, that he rarely did this when anyone other than his immediate staff or family might see him.

Myasthenia gravis can be fatal, but with proper drug therapy and care, many of its victims live a normal life span. The chief danger, and the one all of Onassis' doctors were most concerned about, is that the disease can weaken the heart. Patients, therefore, have to be watched closely and examined frequently. For months, Onassis was in and out of hospitals in Europe and the United States.

The disease makes its victims feel very tired, sometimes very weak. Onassis quickly discovered that he simply could not accomplish as many tasks in a regular day as he had before, and it was now necessary for him to sleep a "normal" eight hours, rather than his usual three or four. But he would not let the illness — or his doctors' orders — curtail his nightlife completely. He continued to frequent his old nightclub and restaurant haunts, in Paris, New York and Athens. More often than not, he was alone. But now he left a little earlier, and often took a taxi to the hotel or apartment he was staying in, rather than walking. Occasionally he even allowed himself to take a short nap during the afternoon.

In October of that year, another death plagued Onassis. His former wife, Tina Livanos Niarchos, died in Paris of a lung ailment. She was forty-five. Her death was so sudden and unexpected, that an autopsy was ordered by Christina. Nothing amiss was determined. She had died from "natural" causes. Coming so close to the other deaths that had affected him so deeply, Onassis felt this new loss might make him crack. But through his own pain, he realized that Christina was truly crumbling under the strain of losing her Aunt Eugenie, her brother, and her mother, all in less than two years. He realized that she desperately needed his support then, and he accepted the heavy obligation to help her through the crisis. It was an effort he hardly had the strength to make.

As Onassis took more time away from his business, he had more time to retreat into his sorrow. Artemis knew he was dying, but the fatal disease was really a broken heart. Everyone close to him sensed the difference in his attitude, his spirit. Each new sorrow seemed to hammer him down more, and he gave no sign of even trying to fight his way out of the depression that had overwhelmed him.

At the end of January 1975, Onassis reluctantly took to a sickbed at the Glyfada villa with a case of influenza, accompanied by a slight fever. After a few days, he began feeling better, and sitting out on his terrace watching his own Olympic planes approaching and leaving the nearby Athens airport, made plans to attend a business meeting with Greek officials and shareholders, pertaining to the government's take-over of Olympic Airways. His doctors attempted almost physically to restrain him from going. It was a cold, damp day and his temperature was still not normal. But however much they argued, he stubbornly refused to listen. He spent the whole day in difficult negotiations, then remained in downtown Athens to have dinner at the Grand Bretagne Hotel, returning to the villa late that night, chilled and exhausted.

It was a costly excursion. His condition weakened rapidly, and within a week, Onassis' doctors were describing him as "seriously ill." It was apparent that his life was in danger—his fever was high and constant, he couldn't eat and his weight was plunging; he slept constantly.

Dr. Isador Rosenfeld, a heart specialist from New York, was flown to Greece to render a diagnosis. He immediately ordered cardiographic and oxygen equipment, and eventually prognosed Onassis' condition as "grave."

Jackie flew from New York and Christina arrived from Paris. Both women, and Onassis' three sisters, sat around his bed, taking turns to make certain that at least one of them would be with him when he woke. They talked with him and tried to comfort him. His conversation seemed somewhat disorderly and inconsistent. He began making pronouncements and value judgments, sometimes seeming to be holding a dialogue with himself. He talked of selling Skorpios; he complained about Olympic; the subject of Tina and Niarchos kept arising—he said they had married to "spite" him. He wanted Christina near him all the time.

Christina became extremely annoyed by the newsmen prowling around outside the house, and at one point she yelled out at them, "Anyone would think we're prisoners being besieged by you!"

Telephone calls, about two hundred a day, began to jam the phone lines. Flowers and gifts arrived from all over the world. The German newspaper *Die Welt* had erroneously published a story saying that Onassis had died on February 5, after having struggled to breathe with oxygen and resuscitation equipment.

The doctors suggested finally that Onassis be hospitalized. Jackie thought the advice was sound but Onassis' sisters wanted him to remain at home in Greece. "He's my husband and I believe this switch is necessary," said Jackie. "Let's not argue." The most logical choice seemed to be the American Hospital in Paris, since their facilities were excellent, and a number of the doctors on their staff, or associated with the hospital, specialized in myasthenia gravis. Onassis' private jet, which had been primed and waiting for days, flew Onassis, Jackie, and Christina to Paris. His sisters flew separately. Always the old war-horse, Onassis waved off the stretcher and left the villa in Glyfada on his own two feet. After arriving in Paris, he would not check into the hospital that night. Instead, he went directly to his apartment on Avenue Foch.

The evening proved to be grim, filled with the pathos of the inevitable. He knew he was dying. Restless and tense, he refused, or was unable, to sleep. He walked through the apartment, back and forth, wraith-like, all night. The cacophony of his sickness was heard during his constant visits to the bathroom. If he were afraid, or in pain, or frustrated at the impending end of his life, or perhaps even seeking death as a release from his sadness and tension and depression, no one knew. But no one else in the apartment slept that night, either.

The next morning he checked into the American Hospital. Within a few days, his gallbladder was removed after he had an attack of gallstones. His condition worsened. As her husband lay dying, Jackie stayed with him, leaving the hospital only in the early evening, having dinner with an old school friend from Vassar who now lived in Paris, and then spending the remainder of the evening back at the hospital.

When Onassis spoke, he talked in Greek, and his sisters and Christina talked to him in Greek. The women began to display an aloofness toward Jackie. It seemed that she represented a symbol of a continuation of the constant tragedy that besieged her first husband's family.

The women were also fully aware that Onassis had

been investigating the possibility of divorcing Jackie. He had discussed it with his sisters. In the fall, just before he became ill, he had instructed Johnny Meyer, in strictest confidence, to talk to one of New York's best divorce attorneys, Roy Cohn, about starting divorce proceedings against Jackie. Although he had told her that there was no further point in remaining man and wife, Jackie hadn't known that he was actually discussing the matter with lawyers.

Meyer told Cohn that Onassis "had had it, that he couldn't take it any more," but also explained that attempts were being made to try to "work things out." The conversation ended with Meyer asking Cohn if he would represent Onassis in the event that "things could not be worked out amicably." Cohn agreed.

Three more consultations took place between Meyer and Cohn within the next few months, two of them by telephone and one at "21" over lunch. Meyer explained Onassis' wishes and the dynamics of the situation to Cohn—Onassis wanted a divorce, but *not* at any price. According to the marriage contract, he would have had to pay Jackie $10 million for every year of their marriage. They had been married for six years; that was $60 million. Even to Onassis, $60 million was a great deal of money, and it assumed symbolic overtones, since one of the chief reasons he wanted a divorce was because of Jackie's extravagant spending habits.

One of Onassis' aides described the relationship at that time as being "totally incompatible." It was eventually learned that when he had argued with Jackie on the plane from Acapulco, he then wrote out his eighteen-page will in which, in effect, he cut her out of his vast holdings.

Jackie was unaware of the terms of the will, but shortly after it had been drawn up, she agreed to sign a separate amendment to her original marriage contract to Onassis, at his suggestion. The terms of the amendment stated that in the event of his death, she would be provided with an income of $200,000 a year for life, plus $25,000 each for her children until they reached their majority. Jackie readily signed the amendment because it was an indication of further security. According to Greek law, widows receive one quarter of the total assets of their husbands holdings. At Onassis death, therefore, she would receive between $125 million and $250 million depending on the worth of his fortune, *plus* the guaranteed income of $250,000 a year, or so it appeared.

Onassis, however, had already manipulated the entire transaction to his favor, giving Jackie only the amount from the trust upon his death and no widow's share of the rest of his money.

He accomplished it as follows: three months after the flight to Acapulco in May 1974, his personal attorney, Stelios Papadimitrou, contacted the Greek Ministry of Justice and met with Minister Stelios Triantailou, one of the junta's most powerful figures. The meeting was held in an attempt to see if the law could be changed to benefit Onassis. Papadimitrou was successful. On June 24, 1974, the Greek Parliament passed a law headed: For the Settlement of Hereditary Questions of Greek Citizens Living Abroad. In effect, the law stated that all marriage contracts concluded and signed outside of Greece, between two parties where one is Greek and the other is not, could not be held as valid, and that the foreigner therefore abdicated his or her rights on the death of the Greek citizen. Eventually, even though the junta collapsed, that law remained on the books and the Karamanlis regime upheld it.

As he lay in bed, his life ebbing away, Onassis undoubtedly worried about his will and who would emerge with most of his vast holdings. He was also afraid that Christina, his principal heir, would not be able to manage his empire alone. She had once been betrothed to Peter Goulandris, a Harvard graduate and scion of another Greek shipping dynasty, but had broken the engagement just before they were to have been married. Onassis had always liked Peter and had been saddened that the marriage had not been consummated. He knew that the young man understood and could mastermind a shipping corporation, possibly even one as large and complex as Onassis'. Softly, he asked Christina to bring Peter to the hospital, and when he arrived, Onassis asked that everyone except Peter and Christina leave the room. The others filed out into the hall, wondering, slightly uneasy or hurt at being temporarily banished.

When Christina opened the door to usher them back inside, she announced that she and Peter would soon be married. Onassis lay back against his pillows, shockingly pale, his weight less than 100 pounds. He could hardly talk, and his vision was blurred and dim. Yet he was smiling.

For the next two weeks, Onassis was closer to death than to life. His heart continued to weaken. He needed the assistance of a dialysis machine because his kidneys were not functioning fully enough, and he was put into an oxygen tent to relieve the strain on his failing lungs. Although he didn't actually rally, he was more comfortable. The doctors said he could linger for weeks, perhaps months.

Jackie flew back to New York to be with her children.

On Saturday, March 15, 1975, with only Christina at his bedside, Onassis died.

Jackie flew back to Paris and upon her arrival gave the press a short, controlled statement:

"Aristotle Onassis rescued me at a moment when my life was engulfed with shadows. He meant a lot to me. He brought me into a world where one could find both happiness and love. We lived through many beautiful experiences together which cannot be forgotten, and for which I will be eternally grateful."

Afterword

The epic life of Aristotle Onassis is as mysterious as a tale from ancient Greek mythology and is a study of paradoxes, altogether gripping because of their seeming inconsistencies.

He was a man so gentle that he could happily play with a child for hours, while corporate executives cried for his attention; and yet he usually bullied, and sometimes physically assaulted, some of the people he loved.

He would spend tens of thousands of dollars to please a friend, but often insulted a waiter with little or no tip.

He had no allegiance to any government, and yet he successfully coped and dealt with every Greek regime during his lifetime.

He had a love-hate relationship with the press, granting long interviews one moment, slugging a photographer the next. He ate in restaurants guaranteed to draw attention to himself, but he was never known to give anyone an autograph.

He had once bought a million ounces of gold; he owned his own Swiss bank; he had plans to build a million-ton tanker; he wanted to inaugurate the first aerial freighter which would fly tourists back and forth to Europe with their cars; he hoped to buy an entire country so that he would never be plagued with taxes; and yet he was known to explode into a fury at being overcharged by two dollars.

He rarely ever gave to charity, but he virtually supported over fifty relatives, and employed over ten thousand fellow Greeks.

He dined and talked with kings and heads of states, but liked to spend most of his time with actors, gamblers, and "just" old friends.

He was born to manipulate, and yet hated to give orders to underlings.

He bought insurance for everything he owned and to cover every eventuality, and yet he claimed that if he lost all his money, he could easily, and without trauma, "start all over again."

He was a man who prided himself in getting everything he ever really wanted in his life, but he was often morose, misanthropic, and acrimonious.

He continually followed one tenet of his own religion at all costs — to fulfill his own well-being; and yet he only truly wanted what he could not purchase — the mercy of the gods.

INDEX

215

217

218